12 EASY STEPS TO SUCCESSFUL RESEARCH PAPERS

Nell W. Meriwether

Printed on recyclable paper

NTC Publishing Group
Lincolnwood, Illinois USA

Sponsoring Editor: Marisa L. L'Heureux
Cover and interior design and art: Ophelia M. Chambliss
Production Manager: Rosemary Dolinski

Library of Congress Cataloging-in-Publication Data

Meriwether, Nell.
    12 easy steps to successful research papers / Nell W. Meriwether.
       p.   cm.
    Includes index.
    ISBN 0–8442–5891–1 (softbound)
    1. Report writing — Handbooks, manuals, etc. 2. Research —
— Handbooks, manuals, etc. I. Title.
LB1047.3.M47 1996
371.3'028'12 — dc20
                                  96–858
                                  CIP

CONTENTS

PREFACE

After more than twenty-five years of teaching students how to write a research paper, I realized that what I really needed to do was to gather all of the information I had taught into a book that could be used by students for many years to come. The result is *12 Easy Steps to Successful Research Papers*, which is a compilation of the ideas I have developed over the years and a gathering of new information having to do with computer research and the like.

Too often the research paper is seen as an overwhelming task. This book is unique in that the directions for writing a research paper are simple enough for even the neophyte writer to understand. By following the step-by-step process explored herein, anyone can write a successful research paper.

In addition to the examples that are provided at each step throughout the book, there are three complete research papers in the appendices. The first research paper (based on *The Grapes of Wrath*) is also the model that is developed step-by-step in the text.

As anyone knows, writing a book takes much time and effort. I, therefore, wish to express my appreciation to my husband, Carl L. Meriwether, for his support and encouragement, and to Cathy Seale, librarian at Tara High School, for her help in gathering information.

Nell W. Meriwether

Steps of the Research Paper

Research paper time has arrived! If you have never written a research paper before, you may think you are facing an insurmountable task. Perhaps your instructor has told you the number of pages you must write, the number of sources you must consult, the number of note cards you must compile, and the job seems overwhelming. You may not have done anything of this magnitude before.

Writing a research paper need not be frightening, though. After you have learned the necessary steps, you may even find it to be an enjoyable challenge. What you will find as you do your research is that other people have thought along similar lines, and you will be able to use their ideas to support yours.

When you have produced the final draft of your paper, you will look with pride at what you have done. After all, it will probably be the first of many research papers you will write either in college or on the job. Thus, what you learn now will be invaluable to you later.

So, welcome to the world of research—a world you will find interesting as well as informative; a world that will become yours by mastering a few simple steps.

The steps you will follow are given below. They are logical and sequential—that is, you should follow them in order. If you follow these steps, you should have little difficulty in writing your paper, and you can see how well the steps fit together.

1. Choose a subject.
2. Narrow the subject into a manageable topic.
3. Research your material.
4. Get information for your bibliography.
5. Take notes on note cards.
6. Form a thesis.
7. Make an outline.
8. Write the first draft.
9. Add the references to your paper.
10. Compile the "Works Cited" page.
11. Revise your paper.
12. Write the final copy.

Step One

CHOOSING A SUBJECT

The first step in writing a research paper is to decide on a subject. Your instructor may give you a specific subject, especially if the paper is on a literary topic. If you may select your own subject, choose a subject that interests you. You may not know much about the subject at the moment, but that's what research is all about—discovering and learning.

FINDING A SUBJECT

If you have not been given an assigned subject, there are several methods that might help you select a subject that appeals to you.

Brainstorming

Think of a subject that you are already interested in and would like to know more about. It could be one of your hobbies or one that you are curious about, a place you have read about or have seen in a documentary on television, or even a culture you find fascinating because of its dress, religion, or customs and foods.

You can brainstorm on your own, or you may want to pool your ideas with other students. Brainstorming with others often brings out many ideas that will help you choose a subject. For example, some of the subjects that members of one class chose were bungee jumping, Himalayan Indian culture and religion, archaeological digs in Israel, AIDS research, and South Pole experiments.

One student, Mike, perked up when he learned that the research paper could be about something of interest to him. He had gone spelunking before in caves in New Mexico, but he had never thought about researching the topic. He immediately chose the subject of spelunking.

Another student, Janice, was interested in stock-car racing. She wanted to find out why there are so few female drivers, so she chose to research that subject.

Because of their previous interest in these subjects, Mike and Janice were ready to start immediately. Other students became just as excited when we began talking about what could be a subject for their research, and their final papers showed their enthusiasm.

Asking Questions

Another useful method for discovering what to write about is to ask friends or family members what they find unusual or interesting. Perhaps someone you know is a member of an unusual group or has a fascinating occupation, such as working as a foreign correspondent, a jockey, or a stunt woman. All of these people started out as ordinary individuals who developed a fascination for unusual occupations. As you talk to them, you probably would want to discover more about their interests, which requires research.

Scanning Books and Videos

If you still draw a blank on what to write, go to the library and look in the indexes of books in an area that interests you. For example, if you are interested in a particular period of history, look in the index of books dealing with history. Subjects such as the Great Depression, the Roaring Twenties, the Harlem Renaissance, or the Reconstruction of the South will stand out. As you scan these topics and others, you will probably be able to find a topic that interests you.

Another place to look for a subject is a bookstore or even a video rental place. Just looking at the titles of books and videos and the placement of them in the stores will often give you a subject to research. For example, Jane was uncertain about a subject. She went to the video store and found one section devoted to children's cartoons. As she looked at the titles, she became interested in what the cartoons were teaching children, because many of them seemed to contain violence. Her research led her to various groups who were advocating censorship of children's programs and cartoons. Jane's investigation proved not only to be the subject of her research, but it also became a project with which she continued to work after she turned in her research paper.

Researching Your Family

Why not research your own family? Instead of the familiar family tree of genealogical research, talk to someone in your extended family who you find interesting for some reason. Perhaps he or she did something unusual or lived in an exotic place. Maybe he or she lived during World War I or II, or helped in the Civil Rights movement, or came as an immigrant from another country during a time of great hardship. Develop your report by enlarging on this particular person and what made him or her interesting.

As you work on this idea, enlarge your focus to include the time period and the problems they encountered, as well as the outcomes of their activities and their effects on your family and even on society. Your paper, then, would not be simply a reporting of your family but would require research of a more objective nature.

Lan, another student, came to America during the Vietnam conflict. On the way over, her father was taken off the boat on which she and the rest of her family were crowded. She never saw him again. Her research project softened some of her bitter memories as she searched her family tree and found men and women who were brave and who dared to stand up for their beliefs.

Lan's paper, though personal, was written objectively. She wrote in such a way that others would want to hear of the bravery and courage of people fleeing a country to freedom to live without the hardships of war.

Writing from an objective point of view is important for a research paper. Using third person pronouns—he, his, him, she, hers, her, they, their, and them, not I, me, mine, we, us, our, and ours—changes the total outlook of your paper so that it becomes less yours and interests more readers.

Another point to consider when choosing a nonliterary subject is to be careful not to narrow your thinking too much. You need enough resources available on your subject for you to do thorough research. The subject must not be too technical for your reader, and it should interest readers besides yourself.

FINDING A LITERARY SUBJECT

Suppose you have been given a literary subject, and you need to narrow it down to a topic for your paper. Let's say the general subject is satire.

As you begin to think about satire, you may remember short stories, novels, poems, or essays that you have read that are satirical. In his poem "To a Louse," Robert Burns satirizes a fashionable young lady with a louse on her bonnet. Samuel Johnson's "Letter to Lord Chesterfield" is a scathing attack on the man who was his supposed patron while Johnson was writing his dictionary. The American humorist James Thurber satirizes people through his caricatures of people behaving like animals and animals behaving like people in day-to-day predicaments.

You may also consider the various forms of satires, such as Juvenalian and Horatian, the origin of satire, or even the use of satire in television and other forms of the media today. The *I Love Lucy* comedy series, which pokes fun at the antics of the American housewife, or *Saturday Night Live* episodes, which use anything and anybody as subject matter, may help you to define your topic. Another option would be to research a modern comic-strip artist, such as Garry Trudeau, creator of "Doonesbury," whose views of social and political issues are shown in his comic strip. You could research the great eighteenth-century British satirist, Jonathan Swift, who wrote "A Modest Proposal," in which he advocated selling babies for food in order to lower the population of Ireland and help alleviate poverty in the country. You could choose John Gardner, a modern humorist who writes using dark or black humor, as he describes the senselessness and meanness of human life in his story of *Grendel,* a retelling of the Old English epic *Beowulf.*

The point is that as you think about the literary subject of satire, or another idea you have developed, your problem becomes one of figuring out what to include because there is so much material rather than not having enough material to research. The next step, narrowing your subject into a manageable topic, follows logically. Before you begin Step Two, however, work the following exercises to practice finding a subject for your paper.

Exercise 1: Library Research

1. Look in an encyclopedia for a subject that you think will interest you.
2. After you have found the subject, determine the time period, if applicable, in which you will be able to find other resources.
3. Next search the card catalog and write down the call numbers of books on this subject.
4. Research the reference section of the library and write down at least three sources that you could use in your search for a subject. These could include print media, such as *The Readers' Guide to Periodical Literature,* or electronic media.
5. From these sources choose one strong subject that you think would be interesting to research.

Exercise 2: Outside Research

1. Go to either a bookstore or a video rental store and write down at least six classifications of books or videos—for example, plays, suspense movies, comedies, and musicals.
2. Choose the one that most interests you from this list.
3. From this classification further narrow the category—for example, if you chose suspense movies, you might narrow the category to Hitchcock suspense movies or remakes of classic suspense films.
4. Then determine a subject you think would be interesting to research.
5. At the library find at least five resources for your selection, using the card catalog and the reference section of the library as other sources.

Step Two

NARROWING THE SUBJECT INTO A MANAGEABLE TOPIC

By now you have a broad idea of your subject. The next step is to narrow it to a manageable size. Narrowing the subject down is necessary because it is impossible to write a research paper on all aspects of any subject. For example, if you were assigned to write about the Persian Gulf War, you would narrow it down to some facet of the war—deaths by friendly fire, calling up reservists to fight, diseases contracted from being in a desert environment, the leadership of the war, or any number of other topics. The whole Persian Gulf War would be too broad a subject to cover adequately.

Narrowing the subject into an appropriate topic helps you to focus in on your research. It gives you a direction to go and keeps you from taking notes on material that does not pertain to your paper. How do you go about narrowing your subject to a workable topic? By following the investigative process below, you will probably find that narrowing your subject into a workable topic is easier than you first thought.

NARROWING YOUR SUBJECT INTO A TOPIC

One of the best ways to narrow your subject to a workable topic is to use research questions. You can develop these through brainstorming or by using the lead questions that are used in journalism: the five Ws and the H—*who, what, when, where, why,* and *how.*

If you are researching a general subject, your questions might look like the following (using the broad subject of spelunking):

1. *What* do you know about this subject already?
   What is spelunking?
   What does it involve?
2. *Who* is involved?
   Who were the first spelunkers?
   Who are some modern spelunkers?
3. *Where* does it take place?
   Where are some of the most well known, largest, or more interesting caves in the United States?
4. *When* did it happen?
   When were these caves or a particular cave first discovered?
5. *Why* is the information important?
   Why is the information gathered by spelunkers helpful?
6. *How* did it begin?
   How did spelunking become a hobby?

These questions do not tell you a great deal by themselves, but they start you in the investigative process. They help you to determine the direction to go, and they give you questions to consider as you begin your research.

You may choose to follow the course of spelunking from early days to the present; you may want to explore one particular cave or one particular spelunker. You may want to incorporate the dangers of spelunking and the safety measures that are used. You may want to investigate what cave exploration has taught mankind and how that information is used in research today. By using this investigative process, you will develop an idea of what to focus on in your paper. In other words, you are now ready to narrow the general subject of spelunking to a more specific topic.

To apply these same questions to a literary subject, you would use the same process. Suppose you have been given the general subject of John Steinbeck's novel, *The Grapes of Wrath*. Naturally, the first thing to do is to read the book, but simply reading the book will not be enough for you to decide on the direction for your paper. The book is the focal point from which to work, but in itself, it cannot be your entire research paper. You will want to research other important ideas you discovered while reading. Investigative questions, such as the following, can be used:

1. *What* is this book's lesson for mankind?
   What different circumstances distinguish these characters from other people who have left their homes and become migrants?
   What caused the government to change its thinking about conservation?
2. *When* was the Dust Bowl that caused such a migration of people?
3. *Where* did the events take place?
   Where did the Okies and Arkies and others come face-to-face with people who feared them because of their sheer poverty and numbers?
4. *Who* was involved?
   Who should bear the responsibility for these conditions?
5. *Why* were these events so important to future generations?
   Why did it take such dire circumstances before drastic measures were taken by the government?
6. *How* did it happen?
   How did people survive with absolutely nothing?
   How did exposing the living conditions of the migrants affect laws designed to care for the land as well as for the migrants?

By using questions such as these, you can see that there is much more to your subject than one book can provide. A host of topics has emerged from reading a single book. Perhaps one topic would be the effect on legislation of Steinbeck's exposure of the conditions of the migrants. Another might be researching the Dust Bowl and its causes and effects, which resulted in the migration of thousands of people to California. You might even consider other books of social protest that have helped to change society; for example, Upton Sinclair exposed conditions in the meat-packing industry in *The Jungle,* which helped to bring about pure food and drug laws. Whatever aspect you choose, your paper will be more thorough because you have investigated many topics that reading the book has opened to you.

You can use these investigative questions for almost any subject. Thinking critically about your subject and asking these questions helps to open your mind to ideas you may have never otherwise considered. To start the investigative process, however, you need to know where to begin—where to find the answers to your questions.

EXPLORING SOURCES TO HELP NARROW YOUR SUBJECT

The two main sources to explore in narrowing your subject are the **card catalog** and the **reference section** of the library. The card catalog contains information about all of the books in the library. The reference section includes reference books, periodical indexes, and electronic sources, many of which contain textual information.

The card catalog is probably the best place to begin your search. Whether it is an electronic card catalog or the traditional version with cards in drawers does not affect your ability to find material. An electronic card catalog, however, is much faster; it can search the library's books not only by title, author, and subject matter, but it can also scan for topics within the books themselves. In addition, it can print out a list of available material so you do not have to write it down.

The reference section is invaluable because it contains indexes of periodicals, such as *The Readers' Guide to Periodical Literature,* and also includes electronic databases. Electronic on-line full-text services are available for your use through these databases. As you research a subject, such as migrants, the Dust Bowl, satire, or spelunking, you can read what other people have already researched on your subject.

Electronic sources, such as Disclit *American Authors* CD-ROM or *Magazine Article Summaries* CD-ROM, as well as non-CD on-line sources are also useful in determining topics to research. In addition, *The Electronic Encyclopedia* and many other reference sets are on CD-ROM. These sources bring up needed information quickly and efficiently, and the research can be printed in a matter of minutes.

The card catalog and the reference section of your library provide necessary resources to help you narrow your subject to a workable topic. And by using the investigative questions while you look, deciding on a good topic will be a fairly simple task.

CONSIDERING AUDIENCE, PURPOSE, AND STYLE AND TONE

As you narrow your subject to a topic, you can make the paper more your own by considering these things: the audience for your paper, the purpose of your paper, and the style and tone of your paper. They will help keep your research focused, and you will be better able to determine how to develop the topic you have chosen.

Keeping Your Audience in Mind

The audience for your paper is a real consideration. If your research is technical, then your terminology will be technical, and you will need to write to an audience who is interested in knowing what you have researched. If your paper involves terms or words that your reader may not understand, consider that as you write and explain their usages so as not to confuse the reader.

The bottom line is that it is always important to keep your audience in mind as you write, even if your audience is only your instructor. One good way to do this is to imagine that someone who knows nothing about your subject will be reading your paper. As he reads it, you can "hear" his reaction to what you have written. If you are sensitive to your audience, you will write with much better clarity and understanding, because you will know how detailed you need to be and exactly what needs clarification.

Determining Your Purpose for Writing

The purpose of your paper is also important as it determines the direction of your research, just as knowing the audience of your paper helps you to make it clearer. Focusing on your paper's purpose also helps you determine the format of your paper to a great degree, as will be discussed in detail later.

If your paper is meant to be a piece of persuasive writing, you will need to include both sides of the argument—the thesis as well as the antithesis. You would want to research both the pros and the cons. Remembering this will help you to narrow your subject to a workable topic.

The same is true with comparison and contrast papers as well as with cause and effect papers. The development of papers using these methods will be discussed in Step Eight. Keeping your purpose in mind as you narrow your subject to a workable topic is important for writing a good paper.

Choosing the Appropriate Style and Tone

The style and tone you use in developing your paper is also a consideration in narrowing the subject. While research papers are more formal than other types of writing, the topic you choose will dictate how formal you will be. For example, a paper that has to do with rap music or radio comedians would be less formal than a paper on the collapse of the Soviet Union.

Style also involves such things as avoiding contractions and personal pronouns in more formal papers. Because your reader relies on sentence structure and word choice to recognize the tone of your paper, sentence variety is encouraged as well as the use of words appropriate to your topic. Clichés and trite expressions are also best avoided. Being aware of the type of paper you are writing helps you to focus your research and to plan how you will develop your paper.

Narrowing the topic, then, is a very important step because it is the foundation on which to build the rest of your research. It determines the direction of your paper as well as the style and content.

After you have narrowed your subject to a topic, the next step is to start your research in earnest. Before you do that, however, practice narrowing your subject to a workable topic by doing the following exercises.

Exercise 1: General Subject

1. Write a list of investigative questions, beginning with:
   Who?
   Where?
   When?
   What?
   Why?
   How?
2. After analyzing these questions, choose at least one topic that has emerged.
3. Research the card catalog and the reference section of the library to find at least five sources on your topic.

Exercise 2: Literary Subject

1. Write a list of investigative questions, beginning with:
   Who?
   Where?
   When?
   What?
   Why?
   How?

2. After analyzing these questions, choose at least one topic that has emerged.
3. Research the card catalog and the reference section of the library to find at least five sources on your topic.

Step Three

RESEARCHING YOUR MATERIAL

Now that you have narrowed your broad subject to a topic you are interested in and feel comfortable with, it is time to start your research. Before you begin, however, it is helpful to plan your research, according to the length of time you have been given for your assignment.

One plan that works well for many students begins at the point where they start their research. In other words, their topics have already been narrowed down. Working within the time frame given, either the instructor or the students work out a timetable similar to the one below:

Tentative Timetable

Possible thesis statement ....End of Week One

Bibliography cards completed....................Beginning of Week Two

Note cards completed ....End of Week Two

Tentative outline ....Beginning of Week Three

Rough draft completed ....End of Week Three

Final copy typed and ready to turn in............End of Week Four

This schedule seems to work well; it allows students four weeks to complete their research paper. Students can add more bibliography cards and more note cards if needed, but the bulk of their work should be done within the time given. Without a schedule students may wait until the last minute, and their papers can reflect their haste. With a schedule they pace their work and do not feel overwhelmed. Four weeks from beginning research to the final draft is enough time for thorough research and writing.

You are now ready to begin your research. If your instructor has not given you a schedule to follow, try pacing yourself by using the one above. You can be much more successful and less stressed out knowing that you are on target with what needs to be done at a particular point.

BEGINNING YOUR RESEARCH

Your school library is the logical place to begin your research, but many other sources are available. Try your city library or a university library if one is nearby. You may also have a state library in which to do research. In addition, ask your librarian about interlibrary loan programs. These are usually available, especially among libraries in your city and even your state. If your library has access to this program, your librarian can help you locate material in other libraries so that you can access that difficult bit of information you need to support your paper.

Another way to find sources for your research in an electronically equipped library is to search other catalogs through on-line services or the Internet. By using these sources, you can immediately retrieve information that is as up-to-date as your daily newspaper.

Understanding the Library

If you are not familiar with the arrangement of your library, trying to find your sources might seem overwhelming. Knowing where and how books are classified is very important. Most libraries, especially school and city libraries, use a method of classifying books called the Dewey Decimal System. Larger libraries, such as university libraries, use the Library of Congress System of classification. By being familiar with both of these systems, you can find your material in either situation.

These classification systems are designed to help you find the books or materials you are looking for. Call numbers (discussed in detail on pages 21–22) are on each card in the card catalog and give you information about how to locate the book. For example, if the number on the card in the card catalog is 331 Min in a library using the Dewey Decimal System, that means the book is in the Social Sciences Section of the library. The number 331 represents books on the subject of Labor Economics. The "Min" indicates the author's last name. The book has that call number taped on the spine. Reference books have an "R" before the number. Books located in other special areas also have a letter preceding their call numbers.

The Dewey Decimal System arranges books according to subjects. If you keep this in mind as you do your research, you probably won't even have to ask directions. The system is as follows:

The Dewey Decimal System of Classification

000	General works
100	Philosophy and psychology
200	Religion
300	Social sciences
400	Language
500	Natural sciences and mathematics
600	Technology and applied sciences
700	Fine arts
800	Literature
900	Geography and history

Each category is subdivided according to the number of books in the system. In our example, 331.1 Min indicates a further subdivision of the subject Labor Economics, with 331.1 representing books on the subject of the Labor Force and Market. Further subdivisions may be needed. You will become accustomed to this system as you look for the books you need and as you become more familiar with the card catalog.

You may also go to a library that uses the Library of Congress System of classification. Just as with the Dewey Decimal System, the books are arranged according to subjects. The difference is that the Library of Congress System is based on letters supplemented by numbers. The Library of Congress System uses twenty-one main categories (the letters I, O, W, X, and Y are not used).

The Library of Congress System of Classification

A	General works
B	Philosophy, psychology, and religion
C	General history
D	World history
E–F	American history
G	Geography and anthropology
H	Social sciences
J	Political science
K	Law
L	Education
M	Music
N	Fine arts
P	Language and literature
Q	Science
R	Medicine
S	Agriculture
T	Technology
U	Military science
V	Naval science
Z	Bibliography and library science

Just as with the Dewey Decimal System, categories are further divided under each broad classification. Subdivisions are organized by letters; subclasses are divided by numbers from 1 to 9999. For example, N is Fine Arts; ND is Painting; ND 1700–2495 is Watercolor Painting. This may sound like a lot to remember, but if you bring this book with you to a library using this system of classification, you should have no trouble finding what you need. Librarians can also help you with your search.

It is best to find as many books as possible on your topic in the card catalog before you begin searching for your material. On a piece of paper or a card, you might list all of the sources you think you need. If you find later that some of them are inappropriate, you can simply cross them off. Then you will not need to go back and forth to the card catalog to find material.

USING LIBRARY REFERENCE SOURCES

Step Two explained the two main sources in the library for your research—the card catalog and the reference collection. Thoroughly explore both of these sources before deciding on one as your main focus of research.

Both the card catalog and the reference collection may be in printed form or in electronic databases. It is to your advantage, therefore, to understand how to conduct research both manually and electronically. A detailed discussion of searching electronic sources follows on pages 23–25.

The card catalog, as pointed out in Step Two, is the place most of you will look first. Whether it is an electronic or traditional version, the card catalog contains an index of all books or materials in the library. The electronic version can let you know which books are available in a matter of minutes. Usually the library will also be equipped with a printer so you can print out the information immediately. If not, however, you may simply write down the information you have found for your topic on a card and then begin your research.

Using the Traditional Card Catalog

The traditional card catalog contains cards listing information about every book in the library, both fiction and nonfiction. There are three types of cards for each book: (1) author card, (2) title card, and (3) subject card. All three types of cards contain the same information, but they are filed according to one of the three headings: author, title, or subject.

The traditional card catalog is set up in alphabetical order with a label on each drawer. The basic information on each card in the card catalog is (1) call number, (2) subject, (3) author's name, (4) author's birthday, (5) date of death if author is deceased, (6) title of book, (7) publisher, (8) copyright date, (9) number of pages, (10) illustrations, if any, and (11) other information, such as maps, annotations, tracing line, Library of Congress number or Dewey Decimal classification.

Call numbers of fiction books contain the letter "F" and usually the first three letters of the author's last name. Story collections are found in some libraries with the letters "SC" and letters from the author's last name. Each library may use its own classification system for story collections, which means they may not all be alike. Browse through the library if you need to use the story collection and find the classification system it uses, or better yet, ask the librarian.

Samples of the author card, title card, and subject card from the traditional card catalog are shown in Figures 3.1–3.3. These cards concern the book *The Grapes of Wrath* because that is the focus of the research paper included in Appendix A.

Figure 3.1
Author
card

F Ste	**Steinbeck, John, 1902–1968**
	Grapes of wrath. Viking 1939
	619p

"Saga of the small farmers and share croppers of the Southwest, driven out of their homes and moving westward with their families and a few household goods piled on a brokendown car. The fortunes of the Joad family, as related here, on their westward trek and after they reach California, symbolizes the whole movement." Book rev. digest

1 California—Fiction   2 Oklahoma—Fiction   I Title   Fic

Figure 3.2
Title card

F Ste	**Grapes of wrath**
	Steinbeck, John, 1902–1968
	Grapes of wrath. Viking 1939
	619p

"Saga of the small farmers and share croppers of the Southwest, driven out of their homes and moving westward with their families and a few household goods piled on a brokendown car. The fortunes of the Joad family, as related here, on their westward trek and after they reach California, symbolizes the whole movement." Book rev. digest

1 California—Fiction   2 Oklahoma—Fiction   I Title   Fic

```
        CALIFORNIA—FICTION
F       Steinbeck, John, 1902–1968
Ste     Grapes of wrath. Viking 1939
        619p

           "Saga of the small farmers and share croppers of the Southwest,
        driven out of their homes and moving westward with their families and
        a few household goods piled on a brokendown car. The fortunes of the
        Joad family, as related here, on their westward trek and after they
        reach California, symbolizes the whole movement." Book rev. digest

        1 California—Fiction   2 Oklahoma—Fiction   I Title          Fic
```

Figure 3.3
Subject
card

Using the Electronic Card Catalog

The official name for the electronic card catalog is on-line public access catalog or OPAC. Some libraries, however, have formed their own acronyms for OPAC rather than saying "on-line public access catalog." Find out what is available in your library, because an electronic card catalog can make it easier for you to do your research.

The electronic card catalog offers the same bibliographic information as the printed catalog. It is also able to search the books in the library not only for the title of the book, the author, and subject matter, but also for many topics or keywords within the books themselves. Each item in the book's record is labeled on the screen, which makes it easy for you to research the particular item you need.

An example of an on-line catalog screen showing the particular areas for research is shown in Figures 3.4–3.6.

The title search screen is shown in Figure 3.4. You would type *Grapes of Wrath* in the blank. The screen will scroll for that title and stop with *The Grapes of Wrath* highlighted in the middle of other entries within the alphabetical range of GRA. (See Figure 3.5.) You would then press the Enter key because *The Grapes of Wrath* is highlighted. The book record is displayed next. (See Figure 3.6.)

The book record shows that the author is John Steinbeck and the call number is F Ste. This library has four copies; three are available, and one has been checked out. The record also shows that there are two subjects under which you could have found the book by using a subject search: "Migrant agricultural laborers—California" and "Labor camps—California." In a matter of minutes, the electronic record gives all of the information you would find in the traditional card catalog.

Doing a keyword search is another option. The example shown in Figure 3.7 demonstrates a search using the keyword "Dust Bowl." As shown in Figure 3.7, it called up the book *Dust Bowl: The Story of Man on the Great Plains* by Patricia Lauber, another possible source to research. The possibilities are almost limitless using electronic sources.

Figure 3.4
Blank title
search
screen

```
Catalog Plus                                          Press <F1> for Help
------------------------------------------------------------------------




















------------------------------------------------------------------------
Title: _____ .

```

Figure 3.5
Title
search
screen
showing
*The Grapes
of Wrath*

```
Catalog Plus                    Title              Press <F1> for Help
------------------------------------------------------------------------
Itms  Title                       Author              Call Number
      Grand Prix championship, 1950—   Pritchard, Anthony.   796.7 Pri    IN
      Grandfather rock: the new poet   Morse, David.         808.81 Mor   IN
      Grandfather stories.             Adams, Samuel Hopkin  B 92 Adams   IN
      Grandfather tales; American-En   Chase, Richard, 1904  398.2 Cha    IN
      Grandfather's broadaxe, and ot   Stephens, C. A. 1844  917.41 Ste   IN
      The grandmothers.                Wescott, Glenway.     F Wes        IN
      Grandmother's secret             Palaiseul, J          615 Pal      IN
  3   Granger's index to poetry
  2   The grapes of wrath
      Graphic arts                                           686.2 Gra    IN
      Graphic arts encyclopedia        Stevenson, George A.  686.203 Ste  IN
      Graphic communication in scien   Guidry, Nels          500 Gui      IN
      Graphic design & visual commun   Cataldo, John W       760 Cat      IN
      Graphology : a guide to handwr   Aylesworth, Thomas G  137 Ayl      IN
      Grasshopper book                 Bronson, W            595.7 Bro    IN
      Grasshoppers and their kin       Hutchins, Ross E.     595.7 Hut    IN
      Grassroot jungles : a book of    Teale, Edwin Way, 18  595.7 Tea    IN
      Graven images : 3 stories        Fleischman, Paul.     SC Fle       IN
      The graveside companion: an an                         364.15 Gra   IN
------------------------------------------------------------------------
          Use / to move highlight, <Enter> to search titles
```

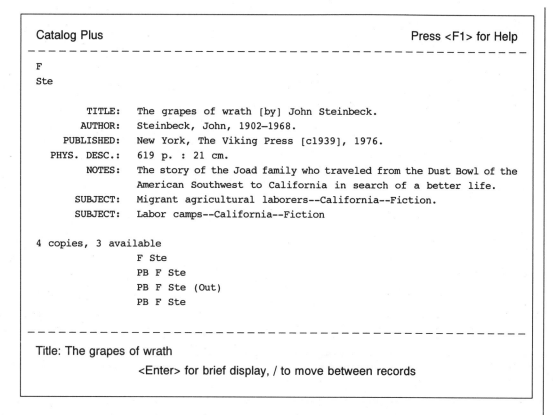

```
Catalog Plus                                        Press <F1> for Help
- - - - - - - - - - - - - - - - - - - - - - - - - - - - - - - - - - - -
F
Ste

            TITLE:   The grapes of wrath [by] John Steinbeck.
           AUTHOR:   Steinbeck, John, 1902-1968.
        PUBLISHED:   New York, The Viking Press [c1939], 1976.
       PHYS. DESC.:  619 p. : 21 cm.
            NOTES:   The story of the Joad family who traveled from the Dust Bowl of the
                     American Southwest to California in search of a better life.
          SUBJECT:   Migrant agricultural laborers--California--Fiction.
          SUBJECT:   Labor camps--California--Fiction

4 copies, 3 available
                F Ste
                PB F Ste
                PB F Ste (Out)
                PB F Ste


- - - - - - - - - - - - - - - - - - - - - - - - - - - - - - - - - - - -

Title: The grapes of wrath

              <Enter> for brief display, / to move between records
```

Figure 3.6
Book
record

```
Catalog Plus                                        Press <F1> for Help
- - - - - - - - - - - - - - - - - - - - - - - - - - - - - - - - - - - -
330.978
Lau

            TITLE:   Dust Bowl: the story of man on the Great Plains.
           AUTHOR:   Lauber, Patricia.
        PUBLISHED:   Coward--McKeown, 1958.
       PHYS. DESC.:  96p. : ill., maps.




- - - - - - - - - - - - - - - - - - - - - - - - - - - - - - - - - - - -

Keyword   Dust Bowl
```

Figure 3.7
Keyword
search

As you use this research tool, you can see the advantages of the electronic method over the traditional method of research. Traditional card catalogs may eventually become a thing of the past because of the efficiency and advantages of the electronic card catalog or OPAC.

Using the Reference Collection

The reference collection is another time-saver. Professors and experts throughout the United States are paid to research and compile material so that you can have it at your fingertips when you need it. After you learn how to use this part of the library, you will understand how valuable it is.

Included in the reference collection are 1) **indexes,** such as *The Readers' Guide to Periodical Literature* and *Magazine Article Summaries, CD-ROM;* 2) **literary sources,** such as biographical reference books, critical commentaries of authors and works, and book digests; 3) **ready reference sources** that include facts and statistics, such as *The World Almanac,* and general encyclopedias and dictionaries; 4) **specialized encyclopedias and dictionaries;** and 5) **electronic sources.** Many of these resources are available in both a print and an electronic format. A short explanation of each of these follows.

Print Indexes.   *The Readers' Guide to Periodical Literature* indexes general references of articles from approximately 130 magazines. Some magazines are published monthly, some bimonthly or at other intervals—in other words, periodically. As this reference's name implies, it is a guide to these periodical magazines.

The Readers' Guide to Periodical Literature is published twice monthly and also has a bound cumulative edition published annually. Like the card catalog, articles may be found under either author entry or subject entry. Subject headings are often followed by divisions or subheadings. Many abbreviations are used, which are explained in the front of each edition.

If you need to find events concerning a specific time, find *The Readers' Guide to Periodical Literature* covering that particular date and begin your research. For current topics and topics of uncertain time periods, first search the latest issue and then work backward. For example, if you were searching *The Readers' Guide* for an article having to do with the Dust Bowl, you would start in the 1996 *Readers' Guide.* You wouldn't find any entries, but should keep looking. In the 1985 *Readers' Guide* there is no entry under "Dust Bowl," but it would refer you to "Okies." There you would find an article under the heading *Okies* entitled "The Okies: Beyond the Dust Bowl." (See Figure 3.8.) You would then need to consult the *National Geographic* of September, 1984, for the article. It might be just what you need, so you would look up the article to see if it will be helpful.

Many schools keep few, if any, old magazines. Because of this, you might be tempted to think that *The Readers' Guide* is not useful, but it can provide you with many sources for your research. Get the information you need about these articles. When you go to a larger library you can obtain the back issues of the magazines you need, and you will save time by not having to look up the same information.

Figure 3.8
Page from
Readers'
Guide to
Periodical
Literature

MARCH 1984 - FEBRUARY 1985

Oil well drilling rigs—*cont.*
  Fires and fire prevention
    See Oil fires
  Safety devices and measures
  Ice to the Arctic [artificial ice barrier made to protect
    mobile offshore drilling rigs in Beaufort Sea] J. Widman.
    il *Oceans* 17:50–1 Jl/Ag '84
Oil well drilling ships *See* Ships, Oil well drilling
Oils, Essential *See* Essences and essential oils
Oils and fats
  See also
    Lubrication and lubricants
Oils and fats, Edible
  See also
    Food—Fat content
    Margarine
    Olive oil
  The fish-oil factor: healthy-heart gift from the sea. L.
    Vaughn. il *Prevention* 36:64–9 Mr '84
Oilseed plants as fuel
  Oilseeds for fuel? *Futurist* 18:59 O '84
Oja, Heikki, and Markkanen, Tapio
  A celebration of Finnish astronomy. il *Sky Telesc* 68:503–5
    D '84
Ojai Valley Inn and Country Club *See* Resorts—California
Ojeda, Ricardo A.
  (jt. auth) See Mares, Michael A., and Ojeda, Ricardo
    A.
OK (Term)
  O.K. the last word. R. H. Hopper. il *Am Herit* 36:118–19
    D '84
Okay (Term) *See* OK (Term)
O'Keefe, Michael
  What will the 1984 election mean for higher education?
    il *Change* 16:12–25 O '84
O'Keefe, Timothy J.
  Institution-wide programs. *Bull At Sci* 40:23s–24s D '84
O'Keeffe, Georgia, 1887–
  about
  View from Abiquiu. J. Kornbluth. il *por House Gard*
    156:150–7+ Je '84
O'Kelley, Mattie Lou
  about
  From memories of country life Mattie Lou O'Kelley
    makes magic landscapes. J. Leviton. il *pors People*
    Wkly 22:73+ N 12 '84
  Paints from Sears. M. Goldman and M. G. Goldman.
    il *por Work Woman* 9:138 F '84
Oken, Lorenz, 1779–1851
  about
  The rule of five. S. J. Gould. *Nat Hist* 93:14+ O '84
Okey, Roberta
  The medium is the message . . . and more. il *Americas*
    36:50–1 N/D '84
Oki Electric Industry Co. Ltd.
  Oki, D. H. Ahl. il *Creat Comput* 10:186 Ag '84
Okies
  The Okies: beyond the Dust Bowl. W. Howarth. il map
    Natl Geogr 166:322–49 S '84
Oklahoma
  See also
    Arts—Oklahoma
    Education—Oklahoma
    Flint Hills (Kan. and Okla.)
  Politics and government
  Down-home budget brawl [J. Jones–F. Keating congres-
    sional race] il *Time* 124:36 O 15 '84
  Target: a House seat [J. R. Jones vs. F. Keating] il
    por Newsweek 104:42 O 29 '84
  Religious institutions and affairs
  Can the church make laws about love? [case of M.
    Guinn vs. the Church of Christ] B. G. Harrison.
    Mademoiselle 90:94 Jl '84
  Is church discipline an invasion of privacy? [ramifications
    of M. Guinn case] L. R. Buzzard. il *pors Christ Today*
    28:36–9 N 9 '84
  Marian and the elders [M. Guinn wins lawsuit against
    the Church of Christ in Collinsville] il *por Time* 123:70
    Mr 26 '84
  A premium price on casting stones [M. Guinn wins
    suit against Church of Christ in Collinsville] *Newsweek*
    103:58 Mr 26 '84
  Suing over a scarlet letter [M. Guinn sues Church of
    Christ for social shunning in Collinsville] M. Starr.
    por Newsweek 103:46 F 27 '84
  Woman wins suit against church that denounced her
    for having sex [case of M. Guinn against Church of
    Christ in Collinsville] il *por Jet* 66:18 Ap 2 '84
Oklahoma Art Center
  Art fills the season in Oklahoma City. il *South Living*
    194:3 N '84

Oklahoma City (Okla.)
  Galleries and museums
  See also
    Oklahoma Art Center
  Prisons and reformatories
  Sheriff Geron Neuenschwander turns out delectable jail-
    house cuisine—for just 22 cents a meal. A. Mezey.
    il *pors People Wkly* 21:73+ Ap 30 '84
Oklahoma cooking *See* Cooking, American
Oklahoma Publishing Co.
  At Oklahoma Publishing, a media baron expands his
    empire. T. Mason. il *por Bus Week* p67–8 D 24 '84
Oklahoma Summer Arts Institute
  Arts on Quartz Mountain. J. P. Forsthoffer. il *Horizon*
    27:62–4 S '84
Okra
  See also
    Cooking—Vegetables
Okuma Machinery Works Ltd.
  A U.S. toolmaker cozies up to its former foes [Houdaille
    talks] *Bus Week* p66 Ap 16 '84
Olajuwon, Akeem
  about
  A $6.3-million question: can NBA life spoil the Dream?
    B. Horn. *por Sport Mag* 75:54 N '84
  Akeem gets his dream, joins Houston and NBA's Rookie
    of Year, Sampson. il *por Jet* 66:47 Je 11 '84
  Akeem looks good, but has lots to learn: coach. *por*
    Jet 67:50 N 5 '84
  Akeem the Dream. W. Leavy. il *pors Ebony* 39:68–70+
    Mr '84
  Akeem the Dream ready to become a nightmare for
    NBA opposition. *por Jet* 66:50 My 21 '84
  Double trouble, Houston style. J. McCallum. il *pors*
    Sports Illus 61:18–21 N 5 '84
  Olajuwon joins Sampson, crowds out Caldwell Jones.
    il *por Jet* 66:47 S 3 '84
  Rampaging rookies. C. Leerhsen. il *pors Newsweek*
    104:121–2 N 26 '84
  Rockets consider trading Akeem after salary talks. *por*
    Jet 66:50 Jl 23 '84
  With Twin Towers Ralph Sampson and Akeem Olajuwon,
    Houston Rockets to the top of the NBA. L. Hart.
    il *pors People Wkly* 22:144–6 D 17 '84
Olbers' paradox *See* Paradox
Old age
  See also
    Aged
    Ageism
    Aging
    Longevity
    Retirement
    Senility
  Another stereotype: old age as a second childhood. A.
    Arluke and J. Levin. bibl f il *Aging* 346:7–11 Ag/S
    '84
  Old age needs a new name. F. Nuessel. bibl f *Aging*
    346:4–6 Ag/S '84
  Psychological aspects
  See Aged—Psychology
Old age assistance
  See also
    United States. Administration on Aging
  Champion of the elderly [work of C. Pepper] M. Sinclair.
    il *pors 50 Plus* 24:37–8+ N '84
  Crisis looms as people live longer. *Futurist* 18:65–6 D
    '84
  Keeping up with Claude [work of C. Pepper] M. Sinclair
    il *pors 50 Plus* 24:23–7 O '84
  State and community news. See issues of *Aging*
  The ten best legislators; ed. by Helene Brooks. P. Simpson.
    il *50 Plus* 24:20–2+ Mr '84
  Washington coverage. H. Cunningham. See issues of *50*
    Plus beginning August 1983
Old age centers *See* Senior centers
Old age homes
  See also
    Nursing homes
  The deer who came to dinner. J. Coudert. il *Read Dig*
    125:66–70 Jl '84
  Fires and fire prevention
  Fire safety standards for rest homes. *Aging* 346:37–8
    Ag/S '84
  Norway
  The spirit of giving [bequest by P. Knutsen stipulating
    wine purchase for old age home residents in Gol]
    F. J. Prial. *N Y Times Mag* p35 D 23 '84
Old English festivals *See* Festivals
Old enough [film] *See* Motion picture reviews—Single works
Old enough to do time [television program] *See* Television
program reviews—Single works

Electronic Indexes.   Many periodical indexes are published in an electronic format. These electronic indexes have many advantages. Instead of your having to search through numerous volumes to find the magazine article needed, the electronic versions of indexes provide you with a comprehensive listing of articles, which can speed your research. A number of the electronic resources also provide either abstracts or full-text material, ready to be printed. This, too, helps make your research faster and more efficient.

Figure 3.9 shows an example using the electronic source *Magazine Article Summaries, CD-ROM.* The subject chosen is again the Dust Bowl. While this source provides abstracts of articles, other electronic sources provide full-text magazine articles. Whichever type of program your library has available, abstract or full-text, both are helpful in researching sources.

As you can see from Figure 3.9a, the search was defined by the keyword *Dust Bowl,* only for the items in that library. Figure 3.9b shows there are seven different articles in seven different magazines. A brief abstract is given of each article to help you decide if they are beneficial to your paper.

This source can be very valuable in saving time. Within a few minutes you have seven sources to choose from that would take much longer to find using more traditional methods.

Figure 3.9 Magazine article abstract, CD-ROM (a) Search screen.

```
Author: Steinbeck, John, 1902–1968
             Use / to move highlight, <Enter> to display record

Search                                  MAGAZINE ARTICLE SUMMARIES FEB 94
– – – – – – – – – – – – – – – – – – Search Screen – – – – – – – – – – – – – – – – – –
               Type the words to look for in the lines below
   Word(s) to look for: dust bowl
           along with:
           along with:
            BUT NOT:


   – – – – – – – – – Limit the search using the following fields – – – – – – – – –


        Magazine name:
       Number of pages:                    (E.G. ">1" for 1 or more pages)
          Date Range:                          (E.G. 9001–9012)


     Search for articles with illustrations (Y):
                 Search Cover Stories only (Y):
   Find only items available in the library (Y): y


   – – – – – – – – – – – – – – – – – – – – – – – – – – – – – – – – – – – – – – –

   F1: help                F2: search              F4: change options
   F7: browse journal list  F8: browse subject list  F9: clear all fields
```

MAGAZINE ARTICLE SUMMARIES   Bibliography   Page 1

1.   UNITED States -- Social conditions -- 1933–1945
      The rise of the common man. By Lord, Lewis; Geier, Thom; et al
      Comments on America in 1933 and the start of its climb out of the
      Great Depression. President Franklin D. Roosevelt's New Deal; The
      blizzard of government programs that were started; Repeal of the
      18th Amendment to the Constitution, enacted in 1920 to outlaw the sale
      of beverages with more than 0.5 percent alcohol; The Golden Age of
      Radio'; Release of Disney's 'Three Little Pigs.' INSET: Down and out
      in the dust bowl.
      (US News & World Report, 10/25/93, Vol. 115 Issue 16, 60th anniversary
      p10, 6p, 4c, 10bw) (0041-5537)
      (The library has this magazine)

2.   DUST storms -- Research
      Dancing dust. By Pennisi, Elizabeth
      Focuses on dust storms. Study of a dust cloud by Carol S. Breed and
      her colleagues at the US Geological Survey, which took place 15 years
      ago; The Geostationary Operational Environmental Satellites (GOES)
      tracking of dust storms; Devastation of the Dust Bowl years;
      Calculations of wind erosion; Article by Dale A. Gillette in an
      upcoming issue of 'Global Biogeochemical Cycles'; More.
      (Science News, 10/3/92, Vol. 142 Issue 14, p218, 3p, 1 diagram, 4bw)
      (0036-8423)
      (The library has this magazine)

3.   ECOLOGY
      Environmental literacy sampler. By Dashefsky, H. Steven
      Defines a variety of terms which pertain to the environment. Albedo;
      Baubiologic; Biosphere; Deadtime; Dust bowl; Gaia hypothesis;
      Styropeanuts; More.
      (Popular Science, Jul92, Vol. 241 Issue 1, p52, 2p, 2 illustrations)
      (0161-7370)
      (The library has this magazine)

4.   PESTS
      Day of the locusts.
      Discusses how the drought of 1988 has led to a plague of grasshoppers
      this year which are destroying crops in western Minnesota and creating
      conditions similar to those of the Dust Bowl 1930's. Controversy over
      pest control measures.
      (Time, 7/31/89, p21, 1/4p) (0040-781X)
      (The library has this magazine)

5.   DUST storms
      The Dust Bowl. By Parfit, M.
      On April 14, 1935 a tidal wave of earth flooded the Great Plains,
      turning wheat fields into what became known as the Dust Bowl. Damage;
      Causes; Eye-witness accounts.
      (Smithsonian, Jun89, p44, 13p, 10bw) (0037-7333)
      (The library has this magazine)

6.   BOOKS -- Reviews
      America, seen from up close. By Gates, D.
      Reviews several new books about life in America, dealing with such
      topics as contemporary life, homosexuals, Amish culture, American
      history, small farms, and the Grand Canyon. INSET: The dust bowl
      revisited (50th anniversary of 'The Grapes of Wrath').
      (Newsweek, 5/1/89, p72, 3p, 3bw) (0028-9604)
      (The library has this magazine)

7.   UNITED States -- History
      [The Okies: beyond the Dust Bowl.]
      Time and improved fortunes mellow the memories of the hard road taken
      by the Okies and others during the Great Depression. From High Plains
      to California, the article follows their trail.
      (National Geographic, Sep84, p323, 28p, 1 map, 1c) (0027-9358)
      (The library has this magazine)

(b)
Annotated
result list
or "hit"
list.

Looking over the list, perhaps articles 5 and 7 seem best suited to your paper. All you need to do is to give these magazines' titles and issue numbers to the librarian, who will find them in the library "stacks"—a term for stored magazines. After the librarian finds the magazines, you can take notes and incorporate the findings into your paper.

These examples demonstrating how to use the card catalogs and the periodical indexes concern a literary subject. However, the same steps apply for any subject—spelunking, the FBI, gun control, abortion, euthanasia, and so on.

If your subject is a current topic, you might also be interested in one of the electronic databases that offer current topics through periodical and newspaper sources. Many publishers now offer these electronic research sources full-text, with the ability to print all or parts of the articles. These include periodical and/or newspaper coverage. Some examples of these sources include:

1. *SIRS* compiles full-text articles of interest on particular topics from both periodicals and newspapers.
2. EBSCO's *Magazine Article Summaries* (MAS), which was mentioned previously, offers full-text coverage of over seventy-five periodical titles and annotated coverage of hundreds more.
3. *Proquest* offers a service similar to MAS.
4. *Newsbank* (similar to *SIRS*) provides newspaper articles on selected high-interest topics from major newspapers around the United States.

Literary Sources.

Biographical print reference sources are another place to go for your research. Perhaps your topic is to discover the reason John Steinbeck wrote *The Grapes of Wrath*; you would use such sources to find material on John Steinbeck himself. The list of these types of reference works includes the *Dictionary of American Biography*, the *Dictionary of Literary Biography*, *Current Biography*, and *American Writers*. Others are *Contemporary American Authors*, *Living Authors*, *Twentieth Century Authors*, and many others. In addition to biographical information about authors, some of these reference works contain critiques of the writers' works. Similar books are also available for British writers and world authors. The literary biographical reference section is often one of the best places to find material about a literary topic.

Because you will need as many sources as you can find for your research on *The Grapes of Wrath*, you might choose to use book digests, such as *Master Plots* or *Book Review Digest*. These books offer summaries of works as well as excerpts from reviews others have written about the books and short critiques of the works. If your research time is short, you may find that book review summaries are invaluable in giving you some insight into your topic. By reading them before you read the books—if that is the focus of your paper—these overall views can help you determine the direction you want to take.

Ready References.   Encyclopedias are also a good source to use, at least when beginning your work, but be careful not to confine yourself only to an encyclopedia. Encyclopedias, by their very nature, must cover so many subjects that they cannot contain the in-depth coverage that you need in your research. It is a good idea to branch out into other works, no matter what you are researching. Allow encyclopedias to direct you to additional material, but do not use them as the primary source for your paper.

A number of different encyclopedias can be found in most school libraries. They are aimed at different audiences, which means you should choose the one most appropriate for you. The depth of your subject will help you decide which encyclopedias can best handle your research. Most schools have *World Book, Colliers, Britannica,* and *Americana,* while some will also have *Columbia Encyclopedia, Chambers' Encyclopedia,* and the *New International Encyclopedia.*

Many encyclopedias are also found on CD-ROM, such as *Information Finder* by World Book, *Grolier's Electronic Encyclopedia* (Academic American), *Compton's Multi-Media Encyclopedia, Encarta, Encyclopedia Americana,* and *Britannica Instant Research System.* These encyclopedias can print all or parts of the articles found on any subject.

Specialized Encyclopedias.   There are a number of single- or multiple-volume works that pertain to different occupations, such as *The Guide to the History of Science* and *Space Encyclopedia.* Another excellent source is *Taylor's Encyclopedia of Government Officials—Federal and State,* published every other year, which provides invaluable information for social studies research. There are even sports encyclopedias for those who need to research sports figures or a particular sport. If you are researching a specialized subject, you can probably find just the right encyclopedia you need pertaining to that topic.

You may also need a general dictionary for information of a broad nature. However, more specialized dictionaries are often needed. *The Dictionary of Literary Terms,* for example, is helpful if you need to research a literary term, such as *satire* or *symbolism.* There are also dictionaries on every subject, as well as almanacs, concordances, yearbooks, and books of lists, such as *The Guinness Book of World Records,* which provide specialized information.

The various kinds of indexes are a good source for research. The Wilson Company has periodical indexes on education, library science, and agriculture. Other indexes commonly used in schools include *Granger's Index of Poetry* and the *Short Story Index.*

Other Electronic Sources.   Some information has already been given about electronic sources, such as *Magazine Article Summaries CD-ROM,* encyclopedias on CD-ROM, and electronic newspaper and periodical sources. In addition, there are other electronic sources, usually in a CD-ROM format. Most can be researched by using keywords, and all or parts of their articles can be printed. The list that follows describes some of these sources and the information they cover.

Subject-Related Sources

1. *McGraw Hill Multimedia Encyclopedia of Science and Technology.* Full-text encyclopedia.
2. *U.S. History on CD-ROM.* Full-text coverage of more than 125 well-known books on American history.
3. *Discovering Authors: 300 Biographies.* Full-text coverage of biographical, general information, career, writing, and critical sources.
4. *The Columbia Granger's Poetry Index* (CD-ROM). Indexes 80,000 poems by author, title, first line, subject, and the anthologies in which they are included.
5. *Scribner Writer Series.* Full-text coverage of American writers, British writers, and others.

On-Line Services

1. Prodigy
2. CompuServe
3. America On-Line

On-line services offer a myriad of options, including many reference research sources. On-line means that the information is constantly being updated and is delivered to the computer by a modem hooked up to telephone lines. As you may already know, most of these services are fee-based, not free.

These services provide access to the Internet, the world's information superhighway. The world of electronic sources continues to grow every day. Perhaps you have a personal computer at home or at school that has access to one or more of these services. Once you have confidence in applying your searching skills, all you have to do is to follow the directions on the screen. Experiment with using these electronic sources. You will probably enjoy finding information in such an interesting way.

As you can see from all the information given in this step, the field of sources for you to research is wide open. Step Three is very important because it shows you the myriad sources you can use for your research. It directs you to information on almost any subject you need to research. Now it is up to you.

As you look in these sources, record the information for your bibliography or source cards that will be used later on your "Works Cited" page. Exactly what you need to record is discussed in Step Four.

Before you go to Step Four, however, try the following exercises to prepare yourself for doing research on your topic.

Exercise 1: Floor Plan of the Library

1. Find out from your librarian which classification system your library uses.
2. Draw the floor plan of the library, labeling the main headings of each section.

Exercise 2: Using the Classification System of Your Library

1. Find a cookbook or a book on car racing using the Dewey Decimal System or the Library of Congress System. Write down its title and the call number.
2. Find a book on abortion or euthanasia and write down its title and call number.
3. Write down the title and the call number of a book of poems by your favorite poet.
4. Write down the title and the call number of a book about a famous athlete.

Exercise 3: Using the Card Catalog

1. Using either the traditional or the electronic card catalog, find three resources for the topic you narrowed down in Step Two.
2. Write down the call numbers for these three sources.
3. Locate these three sources, using the call numbers you wrote down.
4. If you are using the electronic card catalog, find the three sources by using either the title of the book or the author's name.
5. Choose a keyword in a book that you might use for research, and call up the material using the electronic card catalog.
6. Print at least one page from this selection.

Exercise 4: Using Other Reference Sources

1. Choose a subject, such as the Indy 500 or your favorite singer. Write down information on at least three magazines with articles about the races or the singer using *The Readers' Guide to Periodical Literature.*

2. Using the encyclopedia, find an article about the "least tern," a bird that is almost extinct.

3. If your library has an electronic periodical index, search for magazine articles on "bionomediation," which is a solution to waste pollution.

Step Four

PREPARING BIBLIOGRAPHY OR SOURCE CARDS

In recent years the term **source card,** instead of the term **bibliography card,** has become popular to identify the references used. Source card is a better term because it says exactly what it means—sources used in your paper. For example, if you use five different sources in your paper, you would list five sources on your "Works Cited" page.

There is no need to list sources that you thumbed through but could not use. A long list of works may look impressive to the untrained eye, but as your instructor reads your paper, he or she can recognize that you have merely listed works and not used them.

COMPILING COMPLETE SOURCE CARDS

The source cards contain the information for your "Works Cited" page, so it is very important to make sure you include all of the material necessary about your sources. The information is basically the same for every reference: title (the book, magazine, or other source), author or editor, place of publication, publishing company, and copyright date. If no copyright date is given, use the initials "n.d." to indicate "no date." You also need the page numbers for your parenthetical notations, but this information will be recorded on your note cards.

Additional information is needed for encyclopedias and other reference works, periodicals, and electronic sources. Because it is important to have all of the information needed for the "Works Cited" page, make sure you write down everything as you do your research. This will save you last-minute trips to the library for that date or author's name you forgot.

Step Ten gives more detailed bibliographic information for the different kinds of references you need to compile the "Works Cited" page. As you are researching, do not worry about a particular form for recording the information on the cards; just concentrate on writing down what is needed.

It is also a good practice to make source cards for every reference you think you might use. If you follow this practice, you will probably have more than enough information at your fingertips and will not have to backtrack as much to find material. It is always easier to put a big "X" over the cards that are not useful and later discard them than it is to go back and search for more information.

As you make your source cards, a shortcut is to number your source cards in the upper right-hand corner of the card. For example, if you have ten sources, you will have cards numbered from 1 to 10. Then, as you take notes, write the number of the source in the upper right-hand corner as well. With this method you will not have to cite the complete reference for where the material came from on the note card. The number in the top-right corner of the note card corresponds to the source card from which you gathered the material. This method is easy to use and is a real time-saver.

The sample source cards in Figures 4.1–4.5 show you how to record the information needed for your "Works Cited" page. They are labeled to indicate which kind of source is used and have a number in the right-hand corner to indicate what your card will look like. The essential information is given: title of work, author(s) or editor(s), city of publication, publishing company, and copyright date.

	1
The Grapes of Wrath Steinbeck, John New York: Viking, 1976.	

Figure 4.1
Source card for a book

	2
Gray, Thomas, "Elegy Written in a Country Churchyard." England in Literature. Eds. Helen McDonald, John Pfordresher and Gladys V. Veidemanis. Glenview, IL: Scott, Foresman, 1991.	

Figure 4.2
Source card for an anthology

	3
Morris, George. "Building on the Past." Sunday Advocate. Baton Rouge, LA 4 June 1995: H1	

Figure 4.3
Source card for a periodical (newspaper)

Figure 4.4
Source
card for a
reference
book

> 4
>
> Gray, James. "John Steinbeck,"
> American Writers "A Collection of Literary
> Biographies." Ed. Leonard Unger. Vol. IV.
> New York: Scribner's, 1971.

Figure 4.5
Source
card for an
electronic
source

> 5
>
> Steinbeck, John. "The Grapes of Wrath."
> Discovering Authors. CD-ROM.
> Detroit: Gale, 1993.

Exercise 1: Making Bibliography Cards

Using the correct format, make a bibliography card from each of the following sources. Number each card in the upper right-hand corner from 1 to 5, because you will be using five sources. Be sure to record all of the needed information, as the same information is also needed for the "Works Cited" page.

1. Book (a novel)
2. Anthology (your textbook)
3. Periodical (a newspaper or magazine)
4. Reference book (encyclopedia)
5. Electronic source (if one is available)

Step Five

TAKING NOTES
AND RECORDING THEM
ON NOTE CARDS

In addition to source cards, two other kinds of cards that you must use in preparing your research paper are **quotation cards** and **summary cards**.

MAKING QUOTATION CARDS

Quotation cards are those on which you record material exactly as it was taken from the source. This means that *anything* that is copied should have quotation marks around it because it is quoted. Students sometimes think that if the material is not an exact statement a person made, such as in dialogue, then it does not need quotation marks around it. This is not true. Anything that is taken directly from the source must be enclosed within quotation marks.

It is also very important that you record the information exactly as written. If a word is misspelled in the quote, write the word "sic" (meaning *thus*) in brackets immediately after the word so your instructor will know that it is not your error. That way you make it clear that you have quoted the material exactly as it was written.

The quotation card shown in Figure 5.1 illustrates how important it is to record exact information. As shown, the number in the upper right-hand corner refers to the source from which the material was gathered. In this case the source was *American Writers,* a reference book. (See source card, Figure 4.4.) The page number is noted in the upper left-hand corner, an easy way to keep track of where the quoted material was found because that information will be referenced in the paper. In addition, the card is titled, which will help immensely when the time comes to sort out the cards and to write the outline.

If you were to use this material in your paper, you would use a form of referencing called parenthetical notation, the form used by the *MLA* (Modern Language Association) *Handbook for Writers of Research Papers.* Simply stated, the term **parenthetical notation** means that the writer

Figure 5.1
Sample
quotation
card

```
p. 54        Joad Family in Flight        4


"Instead of one central figure there is the
family of the Joads, dispossessed tenant farmers
of Oklahoma who take to the highway in a col-
lapsing truck. These people are in flight from
danger even as Odysseus was; they too, are try-
ing to find their way home, to a new home which
will give them a secure way of life and enable
them to achieve dignity. The encounters they
have along the way--across the desert, toward
the orchards and growing fields of California--
are not merely random adventures but the
meaningful events of a vigorous struggle for
survival."
```

will include the page numbers and/or the author in parentheses after the citation. If you were to introduce the quote by giving the author's name, only the page number of the material cited would be included in the parentheses at the end of the quote. However, if you do not introduce the quote with the author's name, you would put his or her name in parentheses along with the page number at the end. Either method works well as long as it blends into the paper. More information is given about parenthetical notation in the referencing section starting on page 90.

MAKING SUMMARY CARDS

Summary cards contain what the name implies — summaries, shortened versions of the material. Summaries are useful for providing the nucleus of your thinking. One librarian suggests that students close their books and then write a summary of what they have just read.

Another kind of summary card paraphrases the work of the writer. These cards are useful, too, and often are more useful than a true summary of the work. With both kinds of summaries, you put the material in your own words rather than simply quote the words of the writer.

When you summarize you do not have to put quotation marks around the summary, but you do need to give credit to the source in your references. If you use keywords or ideas within the summary, however, they should be enclosed with quotation marks because they are not yours. They belong to the author, and you must give him or her credit. The summary card shown in Figure 5.2, using the same information as the quotation card in Figure 5.1, demonstrates how to summarize.

```
p. 54          Joad Family in Flight              4

Rather than emphasizing one character in his
novel, John Steinbeck shows the struggles of the
whole Joad family to survive. Tenant farmers,
they leave their home in Oklahoma in hopes of
finding a better and more secure life in Cali-
fornia, in turn facing one danger after another.
```

Figure 5.2
Sample
summary
card

As you can see from the card, the essential information from the quotation card is there, but it is said in a shortened form in the researcher's own words. In introducing this quote, you might begin by saying something like this:

According to Gray, John Steinbeck uses the whole Joad family of tenant farmers rather than one character to show their struggles as they leave their homes in Oklahoma and make the dangerous journey to California. Here they hoped to find a better way of life that would provide security (54).

By introducing the summary in this way, you would give credit to the person who wrote the article, but, because the selection was summarized, it did not need quotation marks around it. You can even rewrite your summary card to blend better with the introduction. As shown, however, the parenthetical notation after the summary indicates where it came from, but there is no need to record the author's name because it was given earlier.

Sometimes, however, students think they are summarizing a passage when they are actually paraphrasing. There is nothing wrong with paraphrasing material, but you should know how to paraphrase. If you do not, you will soon begin to plagiarize, and that is a serious offense. To **plagiarize** means to take the writings of another person and to use them as your own, whereas to **paraphrase** means *to state the meaning of the passage in other words*. This means that you retain the idea of the writer, but you state it in your own words. A paraphrase is usually about the same length as the original and often follows the original line for line. The difference is that you have used your words rather than the author's.

The sample card in Figure 5.3 shows a paraphrase of the material quoted in Figure 5.1 and summarized in Figure 5.2. The paraphrase follows the original quote almost line for line, using the researcher's own words yet retaining the sense of the passage and the style of the writer.

When putting the paraphrased material in your paper, though, do as you did with the summary card: Give credit to the writer. Either introduce the paraphrase with his or her name and put the page number in parentheses at the end, or put both his or her name and the page number in the parentheses at the end. Because you used the writer's ideas and form of writing, credit is due to him or her. In this way, you avoid plagiarizing or stealing another person's work.

```
p. 54          Joad Family in Flight                4

Steinbeck uses the complete Joad family instead
of one main character to show how the sharecrop
farmers from Oklahoma survived as they left
their homes in a dilapidated truck headed for
California. The Joads were running from danger
and running to what they hoped would be a new
home that would help them to have some self-
esteem and a feeling of security. As they made
their trek across the desert to the land of
their dreams, they had many eventful experiences
which gave new meaning to the term "survival of
the fittest."
```

Figure 5.3
Sample
summary
card (using
paraphrase)

UNDERSTANDING PLAGIARISM

As mentioned earlier students sometimes plagiarize in their papers, often without meaning to do so. Lack of intent, however, does not excuse those who plagiarize. In recent years a politician who was running for a high public office had to step down because someone discovered he had plagiarized in a college research paper, even though it happened more than twenty years before. To say it was done inadvertently did not carry much weight; it is still considered dishonest. Another case in recent years involved a Harvard professor who resigned for the same reason, and in still another case much publicity was given to a prelaw student who failed to properly attribute a source she used in her research paper. She had not put quotation marks around the material but had referred to the passage in her footnotes. Princeton denied her diploma because she had, in effect, said the material was a paraphrase or were her own words by leaving off the quotation marks. Law schools to which she had applied were also notified.

Plagiarism is immoral; it is the same thing as stealing from another person, because you are stealing that person's words. On college campuses plagiarism is called premeditated dishonesty, and the penalty is more severe than cheating on a test. In most schools, this offense means permanent expulsion. No matter how ethical or honest you become later, you would still be denied access to that particular university. Plagiarism is not condoned by anyone; it is a serious offense.

Following is an example taken from *The Grapes of Wrath* giving correct attribution to the source. Below it is an example of plagiarism of the same source. Perhaps by seeing both samples, you will see what is meant by plagiarism.

Correctly Quoting Material

John Steinbeck well describes the scene of the
poor tenants' lands as they are being taken away
from them by the banks:

> The man sitting in the iron seat did
> not look like a man; gloved, goggled,
> rubber dust mask over nose and mouth,
> he was part of the monster, a robot in
> the seat. The thunder of the cylinders
> sounded through the country, became one
> with the air and the earth, so that
> earth and air muttered in sympathetic
> vibration. The driver could not control
> it--straight across the country it
> went, cutting through a dozen farms
> and straight back. . . . He could not
> see the land as it was, he could not
> smell the land as it smelled; his feet
> did not stamp the clods or feel the
> warmth and power of the earth. He sat
> in an iron seat and stepped on iron
> pedals. . . . He loved the land no more
> than the bank loved the land (41).

You may have noticed that there were no quotation marks around the long quote; the indentation shows that it is a quote. The introduction also states the author's name, which makes it unnecessary to give the author's name within the parentheses at the end.

Incorrectly Quoting Material, or Plagiarizing

```
       The tenants in The Grapes of Wrath were
devastated by what was happening to their land
as it was being taken over by the bank. Their
description of the man on the tractor was that
he looked like a monster or a robot. The tractor
he was driving sounded like thunder so that the
earth vibrated. The driver went from one farm to
the other, and it didn't matter to him what
happened, because he could not see or smell the
land as the tenants did. All he did was to sit
on the driver's seat and step on the pedals,
both made of iron. He didn't care any more for
the land than the bank.
```

This example clearly illustrates that the writer is using the same material, changed only slightly. Many of the same words or images are used. The writer has paraphrased Steinbeck's description of the scene. It would have been legitimate to record the material in this manner if a reference were given to Steinbeck. But if the writer does not give credit to Steinbeck, he or she is simply plagiarizing, taking credit that belongs to the author.

The rules for avoiding plagiarism are easy to follow, but if they are not used, you can get into a lot of trouble. It is to your advantage to learn the rules and abide by them. Then you do not have to worry about committing the crime of stealing another person's words.

The following succinct rules are listed to make it easier for you to know how to avoid plagiarizing.

Avoiding Plagiarism

The following guidelines can help you avoid plagiarism problems:

1. *Always* put quotation marks around any direct statement from someone else's work.
2. Give credit to the author for any *paraphrase* of his or her ideas or statements, even though quotation marks are not used, because these ideas are clearly not your own.
3. Reference any material, ideas, or thoughts you found in a specific source if it is evident that they came from your reading and are not common knowledge.

4. Do not reference material that is **common knowledge.** This refers to biographical material such as birthplace, date of birth, death, and other general knowledge. The statement "Skin cancer is caused by too much exposure to the rays of the sun and may not be noticed for years," is an example of information that is common knowledge.
5. Reference any summary—even if it is in your own words— of a discussion from one of your sources.
6. Reference any charts, graphs, or tables that are created by others or that you make with someone else's information. Put the reference immediately below the title of the chart, graph, or table.

Though a detailed discussion of plagiarism may seem irrelevant at this point, it is very significant. If you start writing your note cards using correct references and quotations, you will not need to worry about what is a quote and what is a summary when you begin writing your paper.

Note cards are a must, even in the computer age when photocopiers and other duplicating machines are available. It is much more time-consuming to have to thumb through reams of material to know what is usable than to use note cards taken from the photocopied material.

If you have a computer, however, you may prefer to take notes on the computer instead of using note cards. This is called a note sheet, and it is more easily read if you double-space your notes.

You would follow the same rules as you do with quotation cards and summary cards and put the same information on the sheet as you would a note card: source number in the top right-hand corner, page number in the top left-hand corner, and subject of the card centered at the top of the page. Only one subject should be included on a note sheet.

Whether you use note cards or note sheets, take as many notes as possible. The more notes you have, the better your paper will be because you will have more material from which to work.

Exercise 1: Quotation Card

Record the information below on a note card exactly as it is given. Follow the rules for referencing (this is source card #3). The bibliographic information is also given, and the quote is taken from page 17.

Cooper, Kenneth H., Controlling Cholesterol.
Bantam Books: New York, 1988.

"Like many mass killers, cholesterol was born into the world under rather innocent, unpretentious circumstances. The earliest known scientific investigation into this substance, which would later be identified as one of the deadliest forces in our bodies, dates back to 1733. In that year, a French scientist by the name of Antonio Vallisnieri discovered that gallstones were soluble in alcohol.

"It shouldn't be particularly surprising that this researcher was fascinated by gallstones: These hard, rocklike sources of pain--which are produced by the gallbladder and may vary in size from a little seed to a hefty plum--were popular playthings at many of the social functions of eighteenth-century French aristocrats."

Exercise 2: Summary Card

Using the quotation from Exercise 1, write a summary in your own words on a note card. Reference the material correctly.

Exercise 3: Summary (Paraphrase) Card

Using the material from Exercise 1, write a paraphrase on a note card. Reference the material correctly. Compare your paraphrase to the original to see if you have put the material in your own words line by line or if you have used more ideas and keywords from the author, Dr. Cooper.

Step Six

FORMING A THESIS

By now you have read enough material to arrive at some direction for writing your paper. You have narrowed your subject down to a workable topic, so the next step is to write a **thesis**, or an objective, for your paper. This means that you are going to present an idea—your thesis—that you will prove through your writing. Everything in your paper will support the thesis, which you will argue from your point of view. While it is recognized some research papers are, for the most part, factual, all of them are persuasive in that you are researching material that will prove your assertion or thesis.

ARRIVING AT A THESIS

There are several things to consider in arriving at a thesis. First, you must decide which approach you will take now that you know something about your subject. One way to determine your approach is to brainstorm ideas you have gathered through your research. Jot them all down, then cross out the unsuitable ideas until you arrive at one you can support with your research. Another way to help you arrive at a thesis is to ask the same questions you used in narrowing your topic: *who, what, when, where, why,* and *how.*

While you might ask the same questions with different types of papers, by exploring them you will be able to hone in on your thesis. For example, if you plan to use an analytical approach in your paper, you will be more concerned with the *what* and the *how* of your subject, and your thesis will reflect that stance. If you choose to develop your paper by explanation, you will concern yourself more with *who, what, when, where,* and perhaps *why.* If you are clearly writing an argumentative paper, you will think more about *why* and *how,* and perhaps *who* or *what.* As you ask these questions, you will develop an objective for your paper that you can state in one sentence—your thesis.

There are no hard and fast rules about how to choose a thesis. Brainstorming ideas or asking the questions—*who, what, when, where, why, and how*—and looking over the material you have researched can help you decide what you want to argue. There are, however, some other things to consider in determining if you have a viable thesis—one that will work well with your subject.

Developing a Sound Thesis

The following guidelines can help you develop a good thesis:

1. A thesis should be one arguable point. Because your point is arguable, your approach to the subject is what you will support in your research paper. Your research is simply gathering material others have compiled to support the point of view you have chosen for your paper.
2. A thesis should not be a question. If your thesis asks a question, the reader has no idea what you are trying to support and what stance you are taking. It must be a declarative sentence.

3. The thesis should be restricted, which means that it should cover only those points you intend to discuss.
4. The thesis should have unity. This means that it will have a single purpose, not a double purpose or two different ideas in your paper. Even with a comparison or a comparison and contrast paper, there should still be one overall purpose or thesis that unites the two areas you are investigating.

Refining Your Thesis

You may find that as you write, your thesis changes somewhat from your original statement. This is not unusual. It is encouraged, in fact, because as you begin to write, your attitude toward your subject may change slightly, necessitating a change in your thesis. This means that you are refining your thesis, cutting out parts that you cannot support and adding others you can support.

A well-stated thesis, however, shows in a single sentence the kind of paper you are writing and what it includes. Because everything in your paper reflects the thesis, it is very important to spend some time thinking about this one sentence that is the nucleus of your paper.

For example, look at the subject of John Steinbeck's novel, *The Grapes of Wrath*, and see what could be a good thesis for it. Because your topic is how the migrants or the Okies—the Joad family—were treated, your thesis statement might be similar to the following.

```
John Steinbeck in The Grapes of Wrath realisti-
cally presents a picture of destitution, anger,
hatred, and prejudice against a minority of
people in the United States, which helped to
bring about measures protecting and/or governing
migrants.
```

It is clear from this one sentence what the paper will encompass. It will show a picture of destitution, anger, hatred, and prejudice toward the migrants and will discuss the measures that were taken as a result of this exposure.

This thesis is arguable; it is not a question, it is restricted to the areas you would cover in your paper, and it is unified. Even though it has two parts—the problems of the migrants and the laws that were formulated from such exposure—it is connected.

Defending Your Thesis

Now that the thesis for your paper has been formed, you need to think about the opposite point of view. Any well-written thesis, because it is debatable to some extent, should have an opposing point of view — called the **antithesis.** By looking at the opposite side, you can determine if your thesis has merit, if it can truly be defended, and if someone can present an opposing argument. The hallmark of a good argument is that you are able to defend it, which means knowing what the opposition might counter in the antithesis.

In determining possible antitheses using the Steinbeck example, you might ask questions such as 1) Did Steinbeck portray a realistic picture of the migrants who were run out of their homes during the Dust Bowl? 2) Were most Midwestern people in the same predicament during the late 1930s? 3) Was it Steinbeck's literary reputation that impressed people with his novel? 4) Can a novel such as Steinbeck's truly change legislation by showing the conditions of the migrants?

By looking at questions that go counter to your thesis, you will strengthen your position. You will recognize that there could be opposing points of view. Next write down one sentence that would be an antithesis to your thesis. For the paper dealing with Steinbeck's novel, the antithesis might look like this:

```
It is evident that Steinbeck shows the terrible
conditions of people in the Dust Bowl who were
trying to find a better life by moving from one
state to another; however, to measure the effect
of his novel on the laws of the land is diffi-
cult to prove.
```

The point of the antithesis is to question whether the book was as effective in bringing about changes in legislation as your thesis supports. It also hints that all people in the Dust Bowl had fallen on hard times, not just the minority of migrants shown by the thesis.

By looking at the opposite side, you have formulated the antithesis. It is not necessary, however, to include the actual words of the antithesis in your paper. Instead, you may refer to it in other words or change it to suit your writing needs. If you do decide to use the antithesis in your paper, it would follow in the paragraph after the introduction. More discussion of the placement and merging of the opposing point of view is given in Step Eight, Writing the First Draft.

Now that you have a thesis and an antithesis and know what you plan to support and how it may be countered, it is time to think about organizing the paper. The note cards you have written will help you organize your subject. If you stack all of the note cards with one subject in one pile and then do the same for other subjects, you can see the form your paper will take. A definite pattern will probably emerge because you have more material on some subjects than you do on others. This helps you determine the major and minor points of your paper. You may also realize that you need to do more research on certain parts. Having to do further research is often necessary and can be seen more clearly in an outline of your paper.

Writing an outline is the next step to take in writing your paper. An outline will help you keep on track and be better organized. It shows you the major and minor points of your paper, and it also shows whether you are needlessly emphasizing some parts because you found more material in those areas. In addition, an outline can help you think logically, showing that certain points naturally come before others and some points are less important than others.

The standard outline format in Step Seven is used by schools and colleges alike. The example outline is the outline of the paper concerning Steinbeck's novel. Now that you are familiar with this paper topic, you can see how it emerges through the outline.

Exercise 1: Forming a Thesis

Look at the quotation you copied for your practice note cards in Step Five and, even though there is little to go on, formulate a possible thesis. Remember the criteria for a thesis as you work.

1. Brainstorm any ideas you can think of concerning cholesterol and jot them down.
2. Write out questions that might help you form a thesis, beginning with *who, what, when, where, why,* and *how.*
3. Use your imagination and write a possible thesis for a research paper about cholesterol.

Exercise 2: Forming an Antithesis

Develop an antithesis or opposite point of view to the thesis you wrote in Exercise 1. Write down at least two points opposing your thesis.

Step Seven

MAKING AN OUTLINE

The outline you prepare will be the guiding force for your paper. You have gathered your material, you have considered it carefully, and you have written your thesis. Now you are ready to put everything in order.

First write down the purpose. Your purpose statement helps you to focus in on the question that you have been considering in your research. It will begin with the word "to" and is designed to prove your thesis. Phrases like the following are often used: *to compare, to prove, to analyze, to create, to determine, to examine, to explore, to show, to describe,* or *to record.*

In the example concerning *The Grapes of Wrath,* the researcher determined that the purpose would be the following:

> *Purpose:* To show that <u>The Grapes of Wrath</u> presents a picture of destitution so realistically that Steinbeck was effective in bringing the plight of the migrants to the attention of the government and bringing about programs to help alleviate their problems.

SELECTING SUBJECT HEADINGS

After you write the purpose, look back over your note cards to determine the subject headings. You might find your paper taking on a different slant after you organize your note cards. As you can see from the sample outline on page 57, there was a stack of cards entitled "Critics' Assessment of the Novel." You may not have planned at the beginning to incorporate this point, but the more you read, the more you could see that it was needed.

Another stack of cards was labeled "Themes," another "Saga of the Migrants," another "Steinbeck's Portrayal of Conditions," and finally a stack labeled "Government/Migrant Problems." You will probably realize that some of the stacks could also be divided after you sort them, especially those dealing with "Saga of the Migrants." These would become subpoints in the outline dealing with the problems the migrants encountered as they made their trek from Oklahoma to California.

The outline is divided into Roman numeral divisions, which are the major points, and then these are subdivided into smaller divisions. The introduction and the conclusion are not subdivided, even though they are included as Roman numerals in the topic outline example.

FOLLOWING CORRECT OUTLINE FORM

The correct form for outlines is straightforward. The first level is the Roman numeral "I," which must be followed by Roman numeral "II" and other Roman numerals if needed. The next division is a capital letter "A" followed by "B" with other letters if needed. The Arabic numeral "1" comes next, followed by a "2." If you subdivided into

smaller units, the lowercase letter "a" comes next followed by a lowercase letter "b." Each level may have further subdivisions. The
important thing to remember about outlines, however, is that *just one
point cannot stand alone.*

The form of an outline may be a sentence outline, a topic outline,
or a combination of these. Whichever form you choose demands consistency, which means that you must keep the points parallel
throughout. Examples follow to show how this is done.

Your instructor may want to see a working outline before you begin
your paper to see if you are on the right track or if you are putting
too much emphasis on points that are not a part of the thesis. Your
instructor may also ask you to turn in a final typed outline with your
paper. He or she may want to refer to the outline while grading your
paper to see if you are doing what your outline proposes.

You have a choice as to whether or not to include the introduction
and conclusion when you write the outline. Just be consistent with the
style you choose.

Topic Outline

```
          A Picture of Destitution Yet Hope
  I.   Introduction
 II.   Critics' assessment of Steinbeck's novel
       A.  Steve Culpepper
       B.  Sally Buckner
III.   Themes in The Grapes of Wrath
       A.  Social injustice
       B.  Man's struggle for survival
 IV.   Saga of the migrants
       A.  Frustration and destitution
           1.  Move to the unknown
           2.  Death of Grampa
           3.  Hunger of families
       B.  Alienation and confusion
           1.  Change in societal structure
           2.  Change in name to Okies
       C.  Anger, hatred, and prejudice
           1.  Encounters with police
           2.  Treatment at Hoovervilles
           3.  Tom's promise to Ma
```

   V. Steinbeck's portrayal of conditions
      A. California Growers Association's refutation
      B. Steinbeck's view of the exploitation of the land
      C. Steinbeck's attitudes toward social reform
  VI. Government's recognition of migrant problems
      A. Senate Committee on Education and Labor
      B. President Roosevelt
         1. New Deal
         2. Civilian Conservation Corps
         3. Home Owners Loan Corporation
         4. Farm Security Administration
 VII. Conclusion

Sentence Outline

A Picture of Destitution Yet Hope

   I. Critics appraise Steinbeck's <u>The Grapes of Wrath</u> as a social document.
      A. Steve Culpepper sees the novel as a monument to the time.
      B. Sally Buckner sees the novel as a vivid portrayal of oppression.
  II. Themes brought out in the novel all point toward social protest and the right to live meaningful lives.
      A. Social injustice is shown through the way the migrants are treated.
      B. Man's struggle to survive involves his acceptance of himself as a part of a whole.
 III. The saga of the migrants is vividly shown through their trials and disappointments.

A. Frustration and destitution are felt as soon as the Joad family is dispossessed of their land.

    1. The Joads are forced to leave their homes and head for the unknown.

    2. Grampa dies before they get out of Oklahoma because he can't stand to leave.

    3. Families are alike as they migrate west with hunger always present.

B. Families are alienated from the landowners as they travel west and are confused at the way they are treated.

    1. The structure of the family changes as they build their own little world at night and travel by day.

    2. The migrants are confused by being called Okies, a name meaning scum.

C. As they travel, emotions of anger and hatred become the norm because of prejudice they experience by townspeople and police.

    1. Police intimidate them by their constant annoyance and surveillance.

    2. Treatment in the Hoovervilles is far from what they had imagined they would find in this land of their dreams.

    3. Tom Joad, as a fugitive, promises Ma he'll always be where there is a need to fight for the migrants' rights.

V. Steinbeck shows conditions realistically of hopelessness and despair, yet he also gives reason for hope.

A. The California Growers Associations refute the picture Steinbeck portrays in his novel.

B. Steinbeck, however, maintains that the land is being exploited at the expense of the individual.

C. Steinbeck's attitudes toward social reform brought about a national consciousness of the situation.

VI. The government began to recognize the problem of the migrants and to offer some remedies.

A. The Senate appointed a subcommittee on Education and Labor to study the problem and offer solutions.

B. President Roosevelt ordered new projects to help alleviate the problems created by the Dust Bowl and to provide help for the dispossessed as well as job opportunities.

1. The Civilian Conservation Corps began a project of reforestation and flood control to help alleviate the situation caused by the Dust Bowl and to put people to work.

2. The Home Owners Loan Corporation lent money to impoverished mortgagors to guarantee the existence of the family home.

3. The Farm Security Administration provided long-term loans at low interest and sponsored cooperative buying.

Exercise 1: Topic Outline

In Step Five, Exercise 1 (page 47), you took a quote from Kenneth Cooper's book *Controlling Cholesterol* and made a summary card as well as a paraphrase of the material. For this exercise, you will work in groups of four, using information from that exercise as the basis for your thinking.

First, brainstorm as many facts as you can about cholesterol. Then sort them according to subjects and subheadings by clustering the ideas together. After you have done this, form an outline of your ideas. Try to come up with four major headings so that each person in the group can develop a major point with subheadings. See that each of your points is parallel in structure and then put them together into a topic outline. Your outline will not include the introduction or the conclusion as a Roman numeral.

Exercise 2: Sentence Outline

Group yourselves in the same way as you did in Exercise 1 and develop a sentence outline having to do with your findings about cholesterol. With this outline, include the introduction and the conclusion as a part of the outline, but do not subdivide them.

Step Eight

WRITING THE FIRST DRAFT

The first thing to keep in mind as you write your first draft is the method for citing your sources. This manual uses what is known as the "MLA style," which calls for parenthetical notation. *The MLA Handbook for Writers of Research Papers* was first developed by the Modern Language Association of America in 1883 and has been updated through the years. It provides valuable guidelines for citing reference sources from books to electronic databases. Recommendations from the most recent edition of *The MLA Handbook* (1995) are used in this book.

In the next step, which has to do with referencing, you will be given detailed instructions about how to put parenthetical notations in your paper. The examples provided in this section use parenthetical notations. They record the essential information for finding the source in the "Works Cited" page at the end of the paper. By seeing how they are used in these examples, you will be able to understand them better as you look at the rules in the next step.

WRITING THE FIRST DRAFT

When you begin to write your paper, sort your note cards into piles according to the divisions of your outline. Because you already know the major and minor points of your paper, you can then incorporate the information from the cards in your paper in the right place. As you use the material from each card, you may want to draw a big "X" on the card to indicate that it has been used.

You may have access to a word processor; if so, you can delete what is unneeded and add material as you write. If you are writing your paper manually, a helpful hint is to write on one side of the page only. That way you can see what you have written without having to turn the pages from back to front.

Because you are using parenthetical notation, be sure to include the author's name and the page reference of the citation in parentheses immediately after the material you are citing. You can fill in the exact information in your next draft. Another good idea is to number the references as you write so that you can easily find where to put them in your paper after you have finished.

While the MLA prefers parenthetical notation and that is the method used in this manual, some instructors may require endnotes instead of parenthetical notation. To use endnotes, put a superscript number, beginning with 1, immediately after the citation. The full reference is then given at the end of the paper on a page entitled "Endnotes." This method will be discussed more completely in the next step.

Perhaps you are wondering how to actually write your paper. There are several methods, but your thesis usually is the clue as to how to develop it. For example, the thesis concerning *The Grapes of Wrath* showed you that the paper would have two distinct divisions. The first part would show what the shocking conditions were; the second part would give the measures taken by the government that resulted from such exposure.

WRITING THE INTRODUCTION

There are many ways to write an introduction. Five distinct ways are given in this discussion, and you can usually find your paper fitting into one or more of these categories. The important thing to realize, though, is that your introduction sets the tone for the paper. It creates interest in your reader and makes it clear you have adequately researched your material. Because of this, carefully consider how you are going to develop the introduction.

In addition, your introduction for a research paper will be longer than only one well-developed paragraph. You may need three or more paragraphs to introduce your topic. In determining how to write your introduction, you also need to consider how to develop your paper. Methods for developing your paper are discussed later in this step.

Before discussing the five methods for your introduction, there are some styles to avoid in introducing your topic. Humorous or "cutesy" introductions are out of place for a research paper. It is not likely that a research paper will be humorous; save humor for a process essay, a personal experience essay, or a classification essay. Beginning writers sometimes like to introduce their essay by asking questions. This is rarely done effectively, but if this style is used with any paper, the questions must be answered within the essay. Asking questions to introduce a research topic is another style to avoid.

The most feasible types of introductions are the inverted pyramid or funnel approach, short anecdotes, the outline approach, quotations, which may also include definitions of keywords or phrases, and comparison/contrast, or comparison only. A combination of these is also possible. Quotations, for example, are possible with almost any form.

Following is a description of each of these types of introductions, accompanied by a sample introduction that could begin the Steinbeck paper included in Appendix A. Consider each of these types carefully before writing your paper to see which one fits best with your research.

Using the Inverted Pyramid or Funnel Approach

The inverted pyramid or funnel approach is probably the easiest method to use, especially if your paper's purpose is persuasive. A research paper is usually persuasive; you want to get your points across regarding the research you have done, and you want your reader to agree with you. With the inverted pyramid or funnel method, begin your introduction with general, broad statements, then work down to your thesis, which is the last statement of the introduction.

The following introduction uses this format. You will notice that it begins with a broad, general statement about writers exposing societal conditions that need to be remedied. Next Upton Sinclair, a writer who has done this with several books, is discussed. The introduction further identifies the kind of writing this is considered, and finally points out that Steinbeck is a master of this art.

The next paragraph continues to work down to the thesis, which has been italicized for your benefit. As you read the completed paper in the appendix, note how this introduction could have been used instead, and it would have worked as well. Keep in mind the broad first statements that work down to the narrow thesis at the end of the introduction, and you can see how this method works.

Example: Inverted Pyramid or Funnel Introduction

Many writers have felt a need to expose conditions in society that need to be remedied through their novels. For example, Upton Sinclair in The Jungle revealed the unsanitary conditions in the meat-packing industry in Chicago, which helped arouse public opinion for investigation and led to pure food and drug laws. He also wrote books attacking the steel, coal, and oil industries. The term for this kind of writing is loosely called a proletarian novel or one that deals "primarily with the life of the working classes or with any social or industrial problem from the point of view of labor" (Beach 327). John Steinbeck, author of The Grapes of Wrath, is considered a master in employing this technique.

Steinbeck saw firsthand the problems of the migrants who had fled the Dust Bowl in Oklahoma and surrounding states and who made their way to California hoping for a better life. According to Ed Cullen, in previewing Steinbeck's Working Days: The Journal of the Grapes of Wrath, Steinbeck saw attacks on the grape-pickers by strikebusters. He saw thousands upon thousands of migrant families in the flooded area in the Salinas Valley, which inspired him to write The Grapes of Wrath (21). *In his novel, he realistically presents a picture of frustration and destitution, of alienation and confusion, of anger, hatred, and prejudice against a minority of people in the United States, which helped to bring about laws protecting and/or governing migrants.*

Using the Short Anecdote Approach

Using **anecdotes** is another way to introduce your paper. People sometimes think anecdotes have to be humorous—and some are humorous—but anecdotes, simply defined, are accounts of interesting incidents or events. Sometimes these are found in newspapers; they may be stories of something that happened a long time ago. Often they give narratives or details about historical figures that make their lives more interesting. Anecdotes make the research paper more interesting because they stimulate the reader to want to know more about what you are writing. If they are used effectively, anecdotes are an excellent way to introduce your paper.

The paper on *The Grapes of Wrath* in Appendix A uses this method. Included in the introduction is the story of a young migrant woman working on a degree in medicine at Boston University's medical school. Following is this introduction for you to see how it is truly an anecdote—a narrative of interesting details that emphasize the purpose of the paper.

Example: Short Anecdote Introduction

An article entitled "She Made Her Dream Come True" in <u>Parade Magazine</u>, May 7, 1995, tells the story of Maria Vega, the daughter of migrant farm workers. Maria says she grew up "with little more than a supportive family and a vision of a better future." Maria had always wanted to be a doctor, but she never thought it was possible (Ryan 18).

Through a program at Boston University's medical school to help disadvantaged youths, Maria is making her dream come true. She says, "It's hard, but I'll do whatever it takes to get through" (Ryan 18).

Maria as a migrant still finds it difficult because of the constant moves her family made as she was growing up, following one season of crops to another. Maria's plight dates back many years. It is most poignantly made visible in John Steinbeck's <u>The Grapes of Wrath</u>, a novel which, according to Paul McCarthy in <u>John Steinbeck</u>, exposed "mankind's grievous faults and failures," alerting mankind to social and economic dangers and forgotten commitments and dreams. He says that "Steinbeck's strongest convictions and passions appear in his fundamental belief in humanity, in his expectation that man will endure, and that the creative forces of the human spirit will prevail" (143).

Steinbeck wrote from experience. According to Ed Cullen in previewing Steinbeck's <u>Working Days: The Journals of The Grapes of Wrath</u>, "Steinbeck came to know life in the migrant camps as a journalist. He saw firsthand an attack of grape-pickers by strikebusters in 1936 in the town of Delano. Five thousand starving migrant families in the flooded country around Visalia inspired the final passages of <u>The Grapes of Wrath</u>" (21). *It is this kind of understanding and empathy that led John Steinbeck in 1938 to write* <u>*The Grapes of Wrath*</u> *in which he realistically presents a picture of frustration and destitution, of alienation and confusion, of anger, hatred, and prejudice against a minority of people in the United States, which helped to bring about laws protecting and/or governing migrants.*

Using the Outline Approach

Using the outline approach in the introduction acquaints your reader with what you will discuss in your paper. Of course, you are not really outlining the introduction; you are simply letting the reader know what your paper is about and the major points you will discuss. In giving you writing assignments, your instructor has probably told you to tell the reader what you will write about in the introduction, then write about it in the body of the essay, and finally tell the reader what you have written about in the conclusion. The outline approach follows this format.

An introduction using this approach to the paper about Steinbeck appears below. As you can see, it follows the above format exactly. It begins by identifying the problem, then informs the reader what to expect in the paper: that Steinbeck wrote from experience, that the problem of migrants needed to be addressed, that Steinbeck showed the injustices these people suffered, and that measures were taken to make changes. It concludes with the thesis as the other types of introductions do. The thesis is italicized again so that you can see how it fits in with the introduction and would be as effective as in the other types of introductions.

Example: Outline Introduction

When an author writes about a social problem, he must either write from his own experience, or he must have learned about the problem through observation and research. Because of his interest, he has a sensitivity to the subject and feels something needs to be done to rectify the problem. During the 1930s, one of the biggest dilemmas was the problem of migrants. Many of the migrants were wanderers, but not by their own choosing. They were displaced because of the Dust Bowl, called by some a "freak of nature," which left them with no means of survival on the land.

John Steinbeck, author of <u>The Grapes of Wrath</u>, felt strongly the problem needed to be addressed. He felt it so keenly that he went to Oklahoma and traveled with a group of migrants as they journeyed to California where they hoped to find a better life. He actually lived in the migrant camps, ate their food, and saw firsthand their tribulations, the social injustices that were dealt them, and their struggle to survive.

Steinbeck empathized with these people, and because of this empathy and understanding, he showed their conditions in his novel, <u>The Grapes of Wrath</u>. *In his novel he realistically presents a picture of frustration and destitution, of alienation and confusion, of anger, hatred, and prejudice against this minority of people in the United States, and by doing so, he helped to bring about laws protecting and/or governing migrants.*

Using the Quotation Approach

Using pertinent quotations in the introduction can also be an effective way to start your paper. While quotations may often be a part of other types of introductions, as you have seen in the sample funnel approach and the anecdotal approach, they can also be used almost exclusively. The writer of the paper feels that the quotations very succinctly say what his or her paper is about and therefore this is the best approach to use. Often with this type of introduction, keywords or phrases are defined or identified because of their importance in the paper.

An introduction to the Steinbeck paper using quotations follows; it also identifies the keyword "Okie" and the phrase "Dust Bowl" which are frequently used in the paper. As before, the thesis appears italicized at the end of the introduction.

Example: Quotation Introduction

Since the beginning of time, there have been some people who have had more and some people who have had less. That has been heightened often through economic conditions over which no one has control. In the United States, the Great Depression, which occurred in the late 1920s and 1930s, brought a problem to the forefront that had not previously been as evident. It was caused by the displacement of thousands and thousands of people because of a drought that brought about the Dust Bowl.

Beginning in late 1933, the wind stripped the farmlands from the Dakotas to Oklahoma, some 300,000 square miles of territory. Wechter says, "blackening the sky at noon, burying fences and machinery and desolating thousands of families; and the erosion of human resources followed the flight of the topsoil" (173).

The people who left came to be known as migrants. Wechter describes them in this way:

> A common sight along the highways of the Southwest came to be that of hungry and bewildered men and women trundling handcarts and baby carriages piled high with shabby household goods, their children trudging behind. Others set forth in ramshackle flivvers, with bedding, water jugs and skillets strapped on for easy access (173—74).

There were so many from Oklahoma that they became known as "Okies." This was not a pleasant term; instead it was a derogatory term indicating that they were the scum of the earth.

John Steinbeck wrote <u>The Grapes of Wrath</u>, a moving story of one family in particular, the Joads, who left Oklahoma and traveled to California in hopes of a better land. Steve Culpepper says:

> . . . the book helped to focus attention on the bitter poverty and desperate helplessness of the Depression's victims, the masses of people who more or less like the Joads were forced by circumstances to leave their homes and to wander through nearly unimaginable suffering. And everywhere they went, they were loudly unwanted, abused, and misused (21).

As Culpepper shows, Steinbeck's book *realis-*
tically presents a picture of frustration and
destitution, of alienation and confusion, of
anger, hatred, and prejudice against this minor-
ity of people in the United States, and by doing
so, he helped to bring about laws protecting
and/or governing migrants.

Using the Comparison/Contrast or Comparison Approach

The comparison/contrast or comparison approach is a method that
effectively shows how two or more similar or dissimilar ideas will be
presented in your paper. In comparing, you show the similarities of
ideas, people, or objects; when contrasting, you show the differences
without the similarities. Not all papers lend themselves to this type of
introduction. With a little thought, however, you may find this an
effective method for letting the reader know what your paper is about.

As you can see from the sample introduction that follows, two writers
and their works—Upton Sinclair and John Steinbeck—are compared.
Less detail is given for Sinclair because the focus is on Steinbeck;
however, the comparison effectively draws the reader to the italicized
thesis.

Example: Comparison Introduction

Two men stand out in the early part of the
twentieth century in America for their outspo-
kenness in addressing problems in society. Both
men wrote books that brought to light conditions
that needed to be rectified. These two men,
Upton Sinclair and John Steinbeck, are credited
with bringing about measures in government to
help the causes they exposed.

Upton Sinclair wrote <u>The Jungle</u>, which was
a passionate condemnation of labor conditions in
the Chicago meat-packing industry. He revealed
the unsanitary practices, and, because of his
exposé, pure food and drug laws were passed.
Sinclair was not content with this exposé; he
went on to write about the labor conditions in

the coal, steel, and oil industries. He attacked the American educational system in one of his works, then went further in writing The Profits of Religion, in which he tried to show that capitalists used churches to make poorly paid people resigned to their lot. Needless to say, Sinclair was not a popular person.

John Steinbeck also met obstacles in writing The Grapes of Wrath. According to Discovering Authors, it "caused a furor of both praise and denunciation. . . . It was publicly banned and burned by citizens; it was debated on national radio hook-ups . . ." (1). Steinbeck was appalled at the economic system; he saw "large-scale commercial and industrial exploitation of the land, and he opposed the continued growth of powerful private interest groups . . . at the expense of individual rights and dignity" (Discovering Authors 1).

Both men saw problems that needed to be corrected, and both men decided to do something about what they saw. By exposing deplorable conditions, both men were able to bring the public's attention to these needs.

While conditions for which Sinclair fought are no longer as applicable, the attention of people today is drawn toward Steinbeck's portrayal of the migrants because of the problem of homeless people in any major city in America. Perhaps a modern writer will do as Steinbeck did with The Grapes of Wrath, and something tangible will be done as a result of his or her exposé. All one needs to do, however, is to read Steinbeck's novel to see how he painted a picture of the migrants so realistically in their frustration and destitution, alienation and confusion, anger, hatred, and prejudice that the government was made aware of their plight and measures were taken to help protect this minority of people.

As you can see from the examples, all five types of introduction could have been used with the same paper. The anecdotal approach was chosen for the final paper (see Appendix A), but any one of the five would have been as effective. They all blend into the thesis, which blends into the rest of the paper.

When you write your introduction, keep in mind that the conclusion should relate to it in some way. After reading about the different ways to write the conclusion, you can decide which one works best with your introduction.

Because your research paper is your own thinking, except when documented, you *do not* need to use such phrases as the following:

"In this paper, I will . . ."
"In this paper, I have . . ."
"I believe . . ."
"I think . . ."

These phrases only weaken your paper. They are signs of a beginning writer; you want your writing to be more sophisticated. It is also unnecessary to use personal pronouns because your paper is written objectively. Leave out *I, me, my, mine, we, us, our,* and the indefinite pronouns *you, your,* and *yours.*

One Student's Introduction

One student, Mona Tyson, was given the general subject of the heath in British literature. After careful study she narrowed her topic to include Emily Brontë's *Wuthering Heights,* Shakespeare's *King Lear,* and Thomas Hardy's *Return of the Native.* Her research was commendable. Her introduction and conclusion are found below, and her total paper appears in Appendix B at the end of this text. As you can see, her introduction uses the inverted pyramid or funnel approach. She used broad statements and worked down to her thesis, which is italicized for your benefit. The purpose of her paper is to show how the heath plays a part in the lives of the characters in the works, both realistically and symbolically.

```
    Each geographical region around the world,
whether large or small, continent or country,
has a portion of land within its boundaries that
overpowers and dominates all others. Examples
```

are the dry, dusty deserts of Africa, the swamplands of Louisiana, and the extreme conditions of Siberia in Russia. These vast and distinctive areas possess individual characteristics that enable each to overwhelm its inhabitants, surrounding lands, and oftentimes nature itself.

These examples give an idea of the role that the heath plays in <u>Wuthering Heights</u>, <u>King Lear</u>, and <u>The Return of the Native</u>. Harold Bloom quotes Hardy in <u>Modern Critical Views</u>:

> The face of the heath by its mere complexion added half an hour to evening; it could in like manner retard the dawn, sudden noon, and anticipate the frowning of storms scarcely generated, and intensify the opacity of a moonless midnight to a cause of shaking and dread (22).

According to Thomas Hardy, author of <u>The Return of the Native</u>, the heath is a barren land, occupying space as far as the eye can see, making its inhabitants who look out upon it during the darkest hours of the night, feel a sense of being trapped, never to escape the ongoing obstacle, and also keeping their minds constantly wondering about the world beyond (56).

Not only Hardy, but also Emily Brontë and William Shakespeare have their own thoughts about the heath. Even though their styles and interpretations differ slightly, it is evident through the selected works that Hardy, Brontë, and Shakespeare share the same feeling. *They emphasize the effect the heath has on the lives of their characters by directly associating it with the characters and their surrounding conditions.*

GETTING INTO THE BODY OF THE PAPER

There are several methods you can use to move from the introduction to the body of your paper.

Using the Con Paragraph

In Step Six, which had to do with forming a thesis, you learned that a good thesis always has an antithesis, which may or may not be stated. This is especially useful in persuasive writing, and while the purpose of your research paper may not be totally persuasive, it must be to some degree. Therefore you would do well to consider the opposite point of view.

If you decide to state some of the opposing points, your **con,** or opposite, paragraph would come immediately after the introduction. It would begin with transitions that show your admission or concession. Such transitions as "it is true that," "admittedly," "certainly," "it is a fact," "while it is evident," and "undoubtedly" are excellent beginnings for con paragraphs.

For you to see how a con paragraph works, an example from the paper concerning *The Grapes of Wrath* is shown below. This is the paragraph immediately following the thesis. The antithesis is italicized to show that it was only a part of the con paragraph.

Con Paragraph

While it is evident that Steinbeck shows the terrible conditions of people in the Dust Bowl who were trying to find a better life by moving from one state to another, however, to measure the effect of his novel on the laws of the land is difficult to prove. On the other hand, as in the case of Maria Vega, perhaps even today his work has a lingering effect on the recognition of the migrant situation, for Maria is able to attend Boston medical school because of a program that helps prepare bright but disadvantaged students for medical school.

This paragraph can help you see that the writer is secure in her thinking that measures were taken concerning the conditions of the migrants and that she has stronger points to make than the antithesis.

As it stands, the con paragraph really serves as a transitional paragraph, making the transition from the thesis to the body of the paper smoother than just "jumping into the paper." If you use the con paragraph, you are ready to write the body of your paper and need to decide how best to do it.

On the other hand, you may have decided not to use a con paragraph with an antithesis and want to develop your paper in another way. There are other options, but again there are definite points to consider.

Using Transitions

The first point to consider in moving into the body of your paper is to make a smooth transition from the thesis to the rest of the paper. A transitional word or phrase at the beginning of the paragraph makes the paper read more smoothly.

For example, one student used the following as her thesis:

```
Accordingly, Shakespeare's plays Julius Caesar,
Coriolanus, and Antony and Cleopatra are unpar-
alleled illustrations of how overambition and
intrepidness lead to the downfall of a political
figure and are still important examples of secu-
lar effigies today.
```

She then moved easily into her next paragraph with the following:

```
With that in mind, it brings about the question,
"Why did Shakespeare have such a great influence
on literature?" The answer is that at that point
in history, his style and characterizational
methods were considered radical and eccentric.
```

The second paragraph continued from there. This excerpt shows you how she moved into the paragraph by using the transitional phrase "With that in mind."

It is important, then, to make a smooth transition from thesis to the rest of the paper, no matter how you develop the paragraph.

Using a Summary

Suppose, however, that you feel that it is very important to write a short summary of the work or works you have read in order to be able to adequately discuss them in your paper. Soon after the introduction is the place for such a summary, and the summary itself should be very succinct. It should not be the bulk of your paper; if it is, your instructor will be immediately alerted that you have done little research.

Using Biographical Material

The same guidelines hold true for material concerning the author's life. If the author's birthplace, dates, family, education, or other biographical information is not significant and has little to do with your thesis, do not include it just to fill up space. If you do use this kind of information, there is no need to reference facts that are considered common knowledge.

In the paper on *The Grapes of Wrath*, it was necessary to establish John Steinbeck's credibility for writing about the migrants. This was accomplished by referring to material from two writers who had researched his life and had found out that he had gone to Oklahoma and lived with the "Okies" on their travels to California. Refer to page 133 in Appendix A to see how this was done. His family, his other works, his education, or other parts of his life were not included as these were irrelevant to the paper. But it was important to establish that he knew firsthand what the migrants were going through, and this was the best way to include such information.

DEVELOPING THE BODY OF YOUR PAPER

After you make the transition into the body of your paper, the next question you are faced with is exactly how you will develop your paper. There are many ways to do this. Choose the one that works best for you, depending on what you want to do in your paper and how you have developed your thesis.

There are six distinct methods you can use to develop your paper. You may also use a combination of any of the six, using one method for developing the main points and another for developing the minor points. Consider all of the ideas given here to determine the best method for your paper.

Using Chronological Order

Anything that is in **chronological order** is done in order of time. With this method, you would trace events backward or forward. This form is particularly suited for biographical or historical studies. It is also beneficial for explaining technical processes that involve sequential steps, so it is useful therefore in scientific studies and in almost any research that demands order in development.

Using Spatial Order

Spatial order is exactly what its name implies—organizing according to space. This is an effective method to use in researching an area. For example, if you are researching dialects in the United States, you might want to organize them into sections of the country. If you are writing about voting patterns in a particular area, this would be a good method to use.

Using Cause and Effect Order

Cause and effect involves starting from the cause and then looking to the effects that caused such a result, or beginning with the effects and working back to the cause. You are therefore using either an inductive or a deductive approach. Logical reasoning is used with the process of an argument or **syllogism** that may or may not be stated. It may simply be understood, but the rationale is evident in your ability to develop the paper. The example of the legislation mandated concerning the migrants uses this order. You could work backward or forward with such a topic. You could show that the cause leads to the effects or work the effects back to the cause.

Appendix A contains a research paper concerning *The Grapes of Wrath* that uses cause and effect development. If you study that paper, you can see how the writer demonstrates the injustices and frustration of these people who had been displaced by the Dust Bowl (the cause), then the poor living conditions en route and in the Hoovervilles and the poor working conditions after they got to California (the effects). The final results were the measures taken to ensure that the Dust Bowl would not happen again and the laws enacted to give the migrants better living conditions. A syllogism for the paper might look like the following:

1. *Major premise:* The Dust Bowl caused thousands to flee their homes in search of employment.

2. *Minor premise:* The migrants were mistreated en route to California and after they got there by the farm owners.

3. *Conclusion:* Laws were enacted to protect the migrants and ensure better working conditions.

Though this syllogism does not appear in the paper, it fits with the research.

Using General to Particular Order

General to particular order can be used when you want to start from a broad generalization and then support it with details. An example might be from F. Scott Fitzgerald's *The Great Gatsby*, in which he showed the 1920s as a fun-loving, carefree time with very little seriousness. You could support this idea with details from the book and perhaps some of his other writings to show how this was portrayed.

Using Particular to General Order

Particular to general order is the opposite idea of general to particular. Using this approach, you would begin with examples and build to the climax. Then you would conclude with a broad generalization summarizing the particulars, pointing to their significance. This is similar to what is done with a persuasive paper; where you state the thesis, give examples and support building to your final, strongest point, and then move on to your conclusion.

Sara Popham's paper about Byron's heroes based on Milton's Satan appears in Appendix C. She uses the particular to general style of writing because she begins with examples and builds to the climax or the final assumption that "Byron based his heroes, not just on a common Romantic theme, but on Milton's Satanic hero in particular, attempting to restate the beliefs that he felt Milton had said only vaguely in *Paradise Lost*."

As stated earlier, the methods for developing the body of your paper can be combined, and Sara does this, as she must. She identifies ways in which Byron's Lucifer and Milton's Satan were similar, but then she comes to her conclusion based on examples she has found in both Byron's and Milton's works.

The body of the paper does not have to be as rigid as one, two, three, but it will take some shape if you plan carefully, as you should.

Using Comparison/Contrast or Comparison

If you choose the comparison and contrast or comparison method, you would come to general conclusions by showing the similarities and/or differences of the ideas presented. This could be done through works of literature, time periods, or authors of similar stature. This method could be employed with almost any subject, whether literary, historical, or scientific.

Appendix B contains Mona Tyson's paper, in which she used the comparison/contrast technique. Her thesis clearly shows that she is going to compare and contrast the three writers—Emily Brontë, William Shakespeare, and Thomas Hardy—and their works. She moves first to Brontë's *Wuthering Heights* and demonstrates how Brontë develops the heath and the feelings of the characters toward the heath. The paper then moves to Shakespeare's *King Lear,* showing how he stresses the effect of the heath on the characters. Mona finishes with Hardy's *Return of the Native* and shows how his characters are affected by the heath. The comparison and contrast method was most effective for this paper because Mona analyzed three works.

WRITING THE CONCLUSION

If you have planned well for your introduction and conclusion, they will fit together like the pieces of a puzzle. Your conclusion ties together what you have written, just as your introduction interested the reader in what he or she was about to read. Your conclusion shows the reader that you have presented your material in such a way that he or she agrees with your argument.

As with the introduction and the body of the paper, you may develop the conclusion in several ways. The conclusion generally is no longer than one or two paragraphs; it is needed simply to draw your paper to a close. Several methods for writing a conclusion and examples of each using the Steinbeck paper are listed below. Consider all of them to determine the one that best fits your paper.

Restating the Thesis

Restating the thesis and then broadening out the subject is a familiar way to conclude your paper. This is the opposite of the funnel type of introduction. In effect, by using this method your paper would resemble an hourglass. The introduction begins with broad statements and concludes with the specific thesis, while the conclusion restates the thesis, then broadens out with general statements.

As you can see from the following example, the conclusion begins with the restated thesis, which was narrow, then broadens out with a quote from Millichap concerning Steinbeck's treatment of the migrants, and closes with today's need for recognizing the plight of the homeless.

Example: Restating the Thesis

Steinbeck's portrayal of the migrant situation--frustration, destitution, alienation, confusion, anger, hatred and prejudice--was a realistic portrayal of life in the late 1930s. Joseph R. Millichap characterizes Steinbeck in this way: "No American writer has better exposed the dark underside of the American Dream nor better traced the lineament of the American Nightmare--and few have so successfully celebrated the great hope which underlies the belief in human potential" (178). Even today man still hears the sounds of Steinbeck's novel drumming on the heartstrings of society with the same beat--to awaken all men to the plight of the homeless, the migrants, and to respond to their needs.

Summarizing the Main Points

Summarizing the main points is another effective way to conclude your paper. This method works well with the outline introduction. In your introduction you told the reader what you were writing about; in your conclusion you are telling the reader what you have written about. This is also an easy way to conclude your paper because you are writing a very short summary of your paper.

The example below shows how a conclusion using this method fits into the Steinbeck paper if the outline approach were used in the introduction.

Example: Summarizing the Main Points

While the Okies were much like everyone else who was displaced during the Dust Bowl, they did their best to pull together and struggled to survive as family units. Their flight from Oklahoma to California was filled with one trial and tribulation after another, as

Steinbeck could so aptly show in <u>The Grapes of</u> <u>Wrath</u> because he experienced their plight. Help from the government was a welcome relief to many who endured the hardships Steinbeck portrayed, and, while some even accused him of Communist leanings, Steinbeck's novel drove home the fact that those who are in need must be cared for by individuals and government alike.

Emphasizing Key Words or Phrases

Emphasizing key words or phrases is another possibility for concluding your paper, especially if these terms were used in your introduction. The words or phrases should be those that stand out as you think about your paper. They bear repeating in the conclusion because of their importance. This format works well with the introduction that uses key words or phrases.

Shown below is an example of this method using the Steinbeck paper. As you can see, the conclusion is centered around words that were repeated throughout—Dust Bowl, Okies, prejudice, anger, hatred, and poverty.

Example: Emphasizing Key Words or Phrases

Though the war may have been the catalyst for raising wages and enforcing a truce between the landowners and the migrants, bitter memories of the past were difficult to erase from the minds of those who had suffered immeasurably the effects of the Dust Bowl. Windswept barren land, blackened skies, and the memories of being forced from their homes were often too much for many of the Okies as they came to be called--the scum of the earth. Poverty, prejudice, hate, and anger took the place of love, closeness, and family ties.

Steinbeck's novel, though set in a time long ago, is still remembered for his portrayal of the inhumanity to man that set those who had

against those who had nothing. It is with some
satisfaction, though, that because of Steinbeck's
portrayal, the government finally took note of
the plight of the migrants and began programs
for their relief.

Using a Succinct Quotation

Using just the right quotation can be an effective way to draw your
paper to a close. You may find a quotation that fits well with one you
might have used in the introduction, or you may choose another that
says what you want to say. Using a quotation helps the reader feel you
have spent time searching for the exact quote to sum up your paper.

The example below uses a different quote from the one in the
introduction, but it draws together the points made in the paper. It also
fits in well with the last paragraph before the conclusion in the paper
in Appendix A.

Example: Using a Succinct Quotation

Joseph Warren Beach sums up his feelings of
Steinbeck's novel in this way:

When people are in distress, you want
to help them. If the distress is so
widespread that anyone's help is a
mere drop in the bucket, you begin to
reflect on the causes. You develop
theories. The people in distress themselves begin to ponder causes, the
rights and wrongs of the case, and
they develop theories. . . . The best
of social philosophies, so far as fiction is concerned, is that which comes
spontaneously to the lips of people
trying to figure out a way through
life's labyrinth. The best sort of
story from the point of view of soci-
ology is one that by the very nature

> of its incidents sets you pondering
> the most fundamental human problems
> (327—28).
>
>   Beach sees the migrants, especially the
> Joads, as persisting through a type of instinct
> for life. Though they suffer immeasurably, they
> are never entirely defeated. While the migrants
> are eventually compensated to some degree for
> their persistence by government recognition of
> their plight, it takes a terrible toll on their
> lives. On the other hand, it helps the reader to
> recognize and respond to his role in the scheme
> of things.

These are four ways to conclude your paper; there may be others that you find just as acceptable. Whatever method you use, however, should show a finality to your paper and should fit well with the introduction. Your conclusion shows the reader that you have concluded your findings and that you have presented them convincingly.

The final example is from Mona's paper. Determine which type of conclusion she uses and how it relates to her introduction. (See page 74.)

> It is also obvious, after extensive
> research, that the characters and their circum-
> stances are directly affected by the heath in
> <u>Wuthering Heights</u>, <u>King Lear</u>, and <u>Return of the
> Native</u>. The heath proves itself to be an invin-
> cible foe against anyone or anything that steps
> into its mighty walls. It is even personified as
> possessing human qualities. Bloom best describes
> the heath in all three works as being "slighted,
> enduring, obscure, obsolete, and superseded by
> none" (<u>Interpretations</u> 122). After close analy-
> sis, it is evident that the heath, that massive
> stretch of wild and desolate land, possesses
> power and strength beyond the imagination.

Mona began by restating her thesis in the first sentence of the conclusion, which is parallel to the way she introduced her paper. She included a quote for emphasis, just as she did in her introduction. She then broadened her statements out to the final sentence, which further emphasized the power of the heath. Mona was effective with her conclusion because of its evident finality. It was clearly evident that this was the end of her paper by the way she brought it to a close.

Following these directions will guide you in writing your first draft. After you have finished your first draft, you will need to add your references. The next step shows how to include the references in your paper.

Exercise 1: Write an Introduction

In the exercises in Step Seven, you outlined a paper that could be written about cholesterol. You formed a possible thesis in your exercises in Step Six. Even though you have not done research on the topic, you know something about it.

Split into groups again and determine the best way to write an introduction for a paper dealing with cholesterol. After you have written an introduction, see which method you used for writing it.

Exercise 2: Write the Body

Continue with your groups and refer to the outlines you made concerning cholesterol. Look back through Step Eight and determine which way would be best to develop a paper with the information you have. Write out the order that you would use to develop your paper and state why you think you could develop your paper best using that format.

Exercise 3: Write the Conclusion

Using the same groups, go back over your information and write a tentative conclusion. After you have written it, determine which form you chose based on the information in this step.

Step Nine

ADDING THE REFERENCES TO YOUR PAPER

Adding references to your paper is not difficult once you understand the process. You already have the information in your note cards and source or bibliography cards. Inserting the references is usually a matter of transferring the material and giving credit to the proper source.

Discussing references is a good place to again emphasize the importance of *not* plagiarizing, which is using someone else's material without giving credit to that person or without documenting it. Step Five gave rules for avoiding plagiarism, which, simply stated, are to put quotation marks around another person's material when citing it exactly and to give credit to the author when paraphrasing his or her material or using his or her ideas. Credit is given by using parenthetical notations, which is recording information about the work in parentheses immediately after its usage (see page 90).

UNDERSTANDING DIRECT QUOTES AND PARAPHRASING

In Step Five, an example was given of the correct use of a direct quote from *The Grapes of Wrath*, as well as an example of plagiarism of the same material. The plagiarism was considered so because the writer used the same material but changed it slightly in order to make it his own. Even some of the same wording was used. In addition, the writer did not note where the material came from; he did not give credit to the author.

Paraphrasing, however, is not the same as plagiarism. It means to put the material you have read in your own words and not in the words or style of the writer. While the paraphrase may be almost the same length as the author's, it generally is shorter. It is also different because it summarizes what you have read.

To demonstrate the difference between an exact quote and a paraphrase of the same material, a direct quote from *The Grapes of Wrath* is given below, as well as a paraphrase and a plagiarized account of the same material. Note that with the paraphrase, a reference is given showing where the material came from, just as with the direct quote. Quotation marks are not used because it is not a direct quote.

Direct Quote from *The Grapes of Wrath*

The man sitting in the iron seat did not look like a man; gloved, goggled, rubber dust mask over nose and mouth, he was part of the monster, a robot in the seat. The thunder of the cylinders sounded through the country, became one with the air and the earth, so that earth and air muttered in sympathetic vibration. The driver could not control it--straight across the

country it went, cutting through a dozen farms
and straight back . . . . He could not see the
land as it was, he could not smell the land as
it smelled; his feet did not stamp the clods or
feel the warmth and power of the earth. He sat
in an iron seat and stepped on iron pedals
. . . . He loved the land no more than the bank
loved the land (41).

Paraphrase of Quote from *The Grapes of Wrath*

The tractor drove across the land devastat-
ing everything in its wake--houses, farms, land,
and even the very lives of the people. The
driver was oblivious to any human suffering
because he was only doing a job, a job that bore
no sympathy for the tenants of the land. And
because he was only doing his job, he cared
little for those whose lives were being torn
from the roots of the land, who were being left
homeless by the machine he drove (41).

Note that with the paraphrase, the idea is there, but the words are
different. The description of the merciless driver of the tractor unmind-
ful of the tenants' lives is shown, but the words are not Steinbeck's.
Even so, a page number is given where the material can be found. This
credits Steinbeck and is not plagiarism. The example below, though,
shows how the same paragraph could be plagiarized.

Plagiarism of Quote from *The Grapes of Wrath*

The tenants in The Grapes of Wrath were
devastated by what was happening to their land
as it was being taken over by the bank. Their
description of the man on the tractor was that
he looked like a monster or a robot. The tractor
he was driving sounded like thunder so that the
earth vibrated. The driver went from one farm to
the other, and it didn't matter to him what

```
happened, because he could not see nor smell the
land as the tenants did. All he did was to sit
on the driver's seat and step on the pedals,
both made of iron. He didn't care any more for
the land than the bank.
```

Note that there is no page number or citation after the paragraph. It is presented as if the material is the writer's own words, not Steinbeck's, which is why it is considered plagiarism. If the writer had put the parenthetical notation (41) after the paragraph and had introduced it earlier in the paper as coming from Steinbeck's book, then it would not have been considered plagiarized. Avoiding plagiarism is as simple as that—giving credit to the person who wrote the material and not claiming it as your own.

ADDING REFERENCES TO YOUR PAPER

Having considered how to use the material you've researched, the next step is to learn how to give credit. The most popular style, which is used in this manual, is called the MLA (Modern Language Association) style and is taken from the *MLA Handbook for Writers of Research Papers*, Fourth Edition. While there are other styles for referencing, such as that used by the American Psychological Association (APA), most English instructors use the MLA form. The *MLA Handbook* uses parenthetical notation for referencing and a "Works Cited" page at the end of the paper to show more detailed bibliographic material of the sources. A discussion of parenthetical notation is given in this step, while information concerning the "Works Cited" page is given in Step Ten. Familiarize yourself with both, and you can correctly insert the references in your paper.

Inserting Parenthetical Notation

Parenthetical notation means exactly what the term implies—notations are within parentheses, indicating where the material was taken from. While this form is straightforward to use, keep in mind that the way you cite the material in parentheses must correspond to the documentation in the "Works Cited" page. For example, if you cited John Steinbeck, because you wrote a paper using his book *The Grapes of Wrath*, you would list him in the "Works Cited" page with other bibliographic information about the book. The information in the "Works Cited" page is listed in alphabetical order, so this entry would begin with "Steinbeck, John."

With parenthetical notation, it is important to be as brief as clarity will permit. Only the information needed to identify the source is necessary. *If the quotation is introduced by the author's name, it is not necessary to repeat the author's name in parentheses after the quote; only the page number or numbers need to be included.* If the quotation is *not* introduced, cite enough of the reference in parentheses after the quote to identify the source. Also remember that the reference should follow the quotation as closely as possible. Rules and examples follow to show how this is done.

Books with Author or Editor.
Use the author's name or the name of whoever begins the "Works Cited" entry, such as the editor or translator. Follow the name with the page number or numbers without using any punctuation.

```
(Steinbeck 39)
```

If two or three authors are given, list all authors in the citation. If more than three authors are given, use the abbreviation *"et al.,"* which means "and others."

```
(Smith and Johnson 103)
(Quinn et al. 56)
```

Multivolume Works.
If citing from more than one volume of a multivolume work, include the volume after the author's name, followed by a colon and the page number or numbers.

```
(Archer 2:2012–23)
```

Literary Works.
If citing a literary work, give information other than or in addition to the page numbers. For example, the citation for a play would include the act, scene, and line(s).

```
(King Lear, 5.5.8)
```

Works Listed Only by Title.
If no author or editor is given, use a shortened version of the title of the work.

```
(Report on Indian Education 3)
```

Complete Works.   Usually when you are citing a complete work such as referring to a book as a whole, the work is introduced in the context. However, even if you do not introduce the work, page numbers are not required (see the example below). In addition, one-page articles or articles in works that are organized alphabetically, like encyclopedias, do not require page numbers in the notation.

(<u>The Grapes of Wrath</u>)

Electronic Sources.   Page numbers are not required for nonprint sources, such as electronic or CD-ROM sources, because none are available. The citation, however, should be similar to citations for books except that "CD-ROM" or enough of the source to indicate that it is electronic should be included in the parentheses. In the example below, "Chavez, Cesar Estrada" was the title of the article, not the author. The article came from *Facts on File World News Digest,* but it is unnecessary to give the complete information in the parenthetical reference.

("Chavez" CD-ROM)

On-line References.   State on-line citations similar to CD-ROM references. Give enough of the title of the citation so that it can easily be found on the "Works Cited" page and include the title of the on-line source.

("Steinbeck, John Ernst" America Online)

When using parenthetical notations, it is important to remember that the citation should not interfere with the readability of the paper. One way to make the paper more readable is to introduce the quote or reference within the text of the paper. This is often done by using verbs that blend in with the flow of the paper. Listed below are ten possible ways to introduce a quote by Steinbeck; there are many others. You will notice they are all introduced by verbs.

1. Steinbeck *says,* . . .
2. Steinbeck *points out* . . .
3. It is easy to see that Steinbeck *is referring* to . . .
4. Steinbeck *agrees* with . . .
5. Steinbeck *writes* that . . .
6. Steinbeck *discusses* . . .
7. Steinbeck *believes* that . . .
8. The subcommittee *declares* . . .
9. The government *insists* . . .
10. Steinbeck *explains* his view by . . .

You may have noticed that only the first example, using the word "says" includes a comma after the word. The other examples do not require commas to make the quotation flow within the sentence. There are other words that could be used as well to make a smooth transition into the body of the paper. By introducing the quote, the paper becomes more readable and is easier to document. Only the page number or numbers need be included in the parentheses after the quote.

A different style of quoting is used for a long quotation of more than four lines. A colon introduces the quote, and the parenthetical citation comes at the end of the quote *before* the period. A long quotation is indented ten spaces on the left and is double-spaced. No quotation marks are used, because the indention indicates that the material is quoted.

The instructions for parenthetical notations may seem hard to remember at first, but they are easier than you may think. They are simply commonsense methods for letting the reader know where to find the sources you used, pointing directly to the sources on the "Works Cited" page. They mainly fall into two categories: introduced quotations or paraphrases that only need the page reference in parentheses after the citation, and those quotations or paraphrases that are not introduced, which require the author's name along with the page reference in parentheses.

Quotations should always be brief and to the point. They are meant to support your research, not constitute the bulk of your paper. When too many are used, the reader may find them cumbersome. They indicate that you have not assimilated the material yourself. Quotes are used to show your research skills and to show how other people agree with your thinking. They are necessary for a research paper, but keep in mind to use them economically rather than to overuse them.

Exercise 1: Quoting and Paraphrasing

Select a fairly lengthy paragraph from an article in the encyclopedia or from another reference source concerning cholesterol. Copy the paragraph into your notebook as an example of a direct quotation. Then try your hand at paraphrasing the quotation. Be careful to use your own words to avoid plagiarizing. Trade paraphrases with a classmate and check each other's paraphrasing.

Step Ten

COMPILING THE "WORKS CITED" PAGE

The "Works Cited" page contains information about each of the references you used in your paper. Sources that you consulted and rejected should not be included. You should not list references that you did not use or cite in your paper.

The "Works Cited" page appears at the end of your research paper and gives complete information about where you found your material. You have already compiled this information on your source cards. Simply organize your cards in alphabetical order according to the author's or editor's last name, then record all of the bibliographic material. The few rules necessary for compiling the page are given below, and examples are given for each of the sources you will probably use.

COMPILING THE "WORKS CITED" PAGE

The following guidelines will help you in putting together your "Works Cited" page:

1. Entries begin at the left-hand margin with the subsequent lines of the entries indented five spaces (or half an inch). All entries are double-spaced.
2. All works are listed in alphabetical order according to the author's or editor's last name.
3. If there is no author or editor, begin with the title of the work. Note that the words *the, a,* and *an* are not alphabetized when they begin a title.
4. Do not number the entries on the "Works Cited" page.
5. Do not give page numbers except for works in anthologies, periodicals, and newspapers. Also, abbreviate all months except May, June, and July.
6. If there are more than three authors, list the first one and add *et al.* (which means "and others") instead of listing the rest of the names.
7. When two books by the same author are cited, use three hyphens in the second entry instead of the author's name. Alphabetize these entries according to the titles of the books.
8. Use the following initials to indicate when information cannot be found: *n.p.* for no place of publication; *n.p.* for no publisher; *n.d.* for no date of publication; and *n.pag.* for no page if none is given. Put these initials in the place where such information is usually found.
9. If a suffix, such as *Jr.,* or a roman numeral, such as *IV,* appears after the author's or editor's name, it should be preceded by a comma.

```
Hollandale, Jerry R., IV.


Jones, James, Jr.
```

10. The essential information for all entries includes the author, the title of the work, the place of publication, the publishing company, and the copyright date. The examples given below show variations of the form to accommodate different sources. By following these examples, you should be able to cite any entry; ask your instructor if you run into an unusual source.

Examining Sample Entries

Book by One Author

Girzone, Joseph F. <u>Joshua</u>. New York: Macmillan, 1987.

Note that the title of a book should be underlined (or *italicized* if you are working on a computer).

Two or More Books by the Same Author

Steinbeck, John. <u>The Grapes of Wrath</u>. New York: Viking, 1976.

---. <u>Of Mice and Men</u>. New York: Viking, 1937.

Two Authors

McCain, Garvin, and Erwin M. Segal. <u>The Game of Science</u>. Monterey: Brooks/Cole P, 1977.

Two Authors with the Same Last Name

Kirk, Clara M. and Rudolf. <u>William Dean Howells</u>. New York: Twayne, 1962.

Editor but No Author

Fisher, Patricia, ed. <u>Age Erasers for Women: Actions You Can Take Right Now to Look Younger and Feel Great</u>. Emmaus, PA: Rodale, 1994.

Two Editors or More than Two Editors

Note: Treat these in the same way that two authors or more than two authors are handled, using "eds." after the editors' names.

No Author or Editor Given

Report on Indian Education. Washington: American
         Indian Policy Review Commission, Task Force
         Five, 1976.

Work in an Anthology

Gray, Thomas. "Elegy Written in a Country
         Churchyard." England in Literature. Eds.
         Helen McDonald, John Pfordresher and Gladys
         V. Veidemanis. Glenview, IL: Scott Foresman,
         1991. 314–15.

Dictionary or Encyclopedia Article

LaSor, William Sanford. "The Dead Sea Scrolls."
         The New International Dictionary of the
         Bible. Eds. J. D. Douglas and Merrill C.
         Tenney. Grand Rapids, MI: Zondervan, 1987.

Note: If no author is given, begin with the title of the article. Also, when citing a familiar reference book, do not give full publication information. List only the edition (if stated) and the year of publication.

"Migrants." The Encyclopedia Americana. 1993 ed.

Multivolume Work

Wester, Janet. "The Return of the Native." 1300
         Critical Evaluations of Selected Novels and
         Plays. Ed. Frank N. Magill. 3 vols.
         Englewood Cliffs, NJ: Salem P, 1978.

Note: Cite the total number of volumes if you use all of them. In the parenthetical notation, the specific reference to volume and page number should be given. For example, (2:101–102).

If you are using only one volume of the set, include the bibliographic information for that volume. Only the page reference needs to appear in your parenthetical notation. If the volume has an individual title, cite the book without reference to the other volumes in the set.

Barclay, William. <u>The Revelation of John</u>. Phila-
    delphia: Westminster P, 1960.

Introduction, Preface, Foreword, or Afterword

Young, H. Edwin. Foreword. <u>Travel Tips from a</u>
    <u>Reluctant Traveler</u>. By Jeannette Clift
    George. Nashville: Thomas Nelson P, 1987.

Newspaper Article

Morris, George. "Building on the Past." <u>Sunday</u>
    <u>Advocate</u> [Baton Rouge] 4 June 1995: H1.

Note: If the city is not included in the title of the newspaper, include it in brackets (not underlined) immediately after the title of the paper.

Periodical Article

Jaret, Peter S. "The Great Snake-Oil Revival."
    <u>Remedy</u>. May/June 1995: 22+.

Note: Because the article is continued later in the magazine with other articles intervening, only the plus sign is used with the page reference.

Review in a Newspaper or Periodical

Goldsmith, Sarah Sue. Rev. of <u>The Hot Zone</u> by
    Richard Preston. <u>Sunday Advocate</u> [Baton
    Rouge] 30 July 1995: 19–20.

Personal Interview

Hightower, James S. Personal interview. 30 July
    1995.

Interview Broadcast on Television or Radio

Blackmun, Harry. Interview with Ted Koppel and
    Nina Totenberg. <u>Nightline</u>. ABC. WABC, New
    York. 5 Apr. 1994.

Television or Radio Program

"<u>Frankenstein</u>: The Making of the Monster." Great
    Books. Narr. Donald Sutherland. Writ.
    Eugenie Vink. Dir. Jonathan Ward. Learning
    Channel. 8 Sept. 1993.

Film or Video

<u>It's a Wonderful Life</u>. Dir. Frank Capra. Perf.
    James Stewart, Donna Reed, Lionel Barrymore,
    and Thomas Mitchell. RKO, 1946.
<u>In the Line of Fire</u>. Dr. Wolfgang Petersen.
    Perf. Clint Eastwood, John Malkovich, Rene
    Russo, Dylan McDermott, Steve Railsback.
    Videocassette. Columbia Tristar, 1993.

Note: Videos, cassettes, videodiscs, slide programs, and filmstrips are
cited like films except that the original release date is given if applicable.
The medium (videocassette, videodisc, slide program, and so on) is also
included before the name of the distributor.

Electronic Source

Periodical Publication

"Chavez, Cesar Estrada." <u>Facts on File World
    News Digest</u>. CD-ROM. 29 April 1993.

Nonperiodical Publication

```
Steinbeck, John. "The Grapes of Wrath." Discov-
     ering Authors. CD-ROM. Gale, 1993.
```

Publication on Diskette

```
Bodyworks 3.0. Diskette. Phoenix: Software Mar-
     keting Corp. 1993.
```

On-line Database

Through a Computer Service

```
"Steinbeck, John Ernst." Encarta. Microsoft Corp.
     America Online. 15 June 1995.
```

Through a Computer Network

```
Alston, Robin. "The Battle of the Books." Human-
     ist. 7.0176 (10 Sept. 1993): 10 pp.
     On-line. Internet. 10 Oct. 1993.
```

Note: The information required for an on-line database source is the author, the title of material (in quotation marks), the title of database (underlined), the publication medium, the name of the computer service, and the date of access. If you cannot find some of the information, cite what is available.

USING ENDNOTES AND BIBLIOGRAPHY FORMS FOR CITATIONS

The preceding pages contain information on how to use parenthetical notations and how to record the bibliographic information on the "Works Cited" page. There is another method for referencing, generally called the endnote style. With it you would use a form of referencing in which the references are numbered consecutively at the end of the paper instead of using parenthetical notations. You would list these references on a page entitled "Endnotes" at the end of your paper, and also compile a list of sources on the following page, the "Bibliography" page.

Sara Popham's paper in Appendix C uses this form. Instructions for this method of citation are not given in this step; however, they are included with her paper. If your instructor prefers this method, please turn to Appendix C for information on how to reference using note numbers, endnotes, and the "Bibliography" page.

A combination of the two forms of referencing is not possible. If you are using parenthetical notation and a "Works Cited" page, do not use the form of referencing using note numbers. If you are compiling endnotes and a "Bibliography" page, make sure not to use parenthetical notation. Look at the two research papers in Appendices A and B for examples of using parenthetical notation and the "Works Cited" page.

Exercise 1: Compiling the "Works Cited" Page

Working in small groups, compile a "Works Cited" page of imaginary reference sources you might have used in the cholesterol paper you worked on in Steps Seven and Eight. Try to come up with titles, authors, and publication information for a variety of types of sources (books, magazines, and so on). Try to list at least six imaginary references. Be sure to use correct "Works Cited" form.

Step Eleven

REVISING YOUR PAPER

By now you have written your first draft and added the parenthetical notations. You have used your source cards to list your sources on the "Works Cited" page. You may think that you have completed the major part of your paper. However, you still have another part to tackle: proofing your paper for errors, then revising it for better style, structure, and organization.

Proofing your paper implies looking at it from an outsider's point of view and making the changes necessary to have a really good paper. Reading your paper aloud can be a good way to "hear" how your paper sounds. It is as if another person were listening and finding places that need additional work.

The best way to proof your paper is to read your rough draft several times in order to catch any errors you have made. Reading it at least three times before typing the final copy is a good guideline. Each time you read it, look for specific things. That way you do not have to spot every error at once. After you have found the errors, correct them and begin the revision process.

Your word processor may have programs to help you check your spelling and grammar. These programs highlight your errors on-screen, which enables you to correct them immediately.

Guidelines follow for things to look for each time you read your rough draft. Now is the time to make any corrections, so check your paper carefully.

FIRST READING: CHECKING FOR SPELLING, PUNCTUATION, AND CAPITALIZATION

Look over your paper for the words you often misspell. Usually, you will misspell them again. Using the dictionary can help you with this check; keep it by your side as you write. If a word looks wrong, it usually is. A spellchecking program can also help you spot misspelled words.

While you are reading your paper for spelling errors, check for punctuation errors as well. Too little punctuation or too much punctuation can harm the flow of your writing. If you have questions about how to use commas, quotation marks, and periods, refer to the punctuation checklist at the end of this step. It shows rules and examples for almost any problem you might have.

Capitalization errors are usually inadvertent. You thought you remembered to capitalize that name, that city, or that street, but you may have overlooked it. In this first reading, pay particular attention to capital letters. Keep in mind that proper names, languages, religions, historical events, periods of time, documents, governmental bodies and departments, titles—of books, articles, reports, poems, plays, short stories, and newspapers—names of television and radio programs, the Deity, the Bible, and proper adjectives all begin with capital letters.

SECOND READING: CHECKING FOR GRAMMAR AND STYLE

With this reading, you will be concerned with *how* you wrote your paper. Look for grammatical errors—sentence fragments, run-on sentences, comma splices, pronoun usage, misplaced modifiers, wordiness, and tense shifts. If your paper is literary, keep in mind that you should use the present tense any time you are writing about a literary work; write as if the work were being written now. For example, "Steinbeck *shows* the horrible sanitary conditions of the migrant labor camps, the Hoovervilles. . . ."

During this reading, also note the use of personal pronouns and avoid them. More sophisticated writing uses the objective point of view. In other words, don't use the pronouns *I, me, my, mine, we, us, our,* and *ours*. Also delete the pronouns *you, your,* and *yours*. These are unnecessary in a research paper because they are indefinite pronouns; save their usage for process or how-to papers.

In addition, this second reading is a good time to look at the flow of your paper, especially the use of transitions or transitional devices. If your writing seems too disjointed or lacks continuity, you may need to find ways to make it read more smoothly by using transitions within sentences and by connecting your paragraphs with transitional words or phrases. Study the list of transitions that follows the punctuation rules at the end of this step to help you make your paper flow better. Also use your thesaurus to find synonyms to substitute for words that are repeated often, instead of using the same words over and over. You will be doing your reader a favor as well as learning new words yourself.

Finally, a careful reading can help you identify weak sentences and faulty sentence structure as well as problems with paragraph development. A good guide to judge a well-developed paragraph is to find the topic sentence, then check the paragraph for support and note the way it concludes. A paragraph should contain only one idea. Paragraphs that are too long are difficult to comprehend, just as paragraphs that are too short are difficult to follow.

The second reading requires more time than the first because of the number of things you are looking for. In a well-written paper, however, these errors have been eliminated. Checking your paper for grammar and style is vital.

THIRD READING: CHECKING FOR CONTENT, ORGANIZATION, CLARITY, AND REFERENCING

Checking your paper for content, clarity, and organizational structure is the final step in proofreading your first draft. Have your outline in hand for this reading. Check to see if your paper fits the points on the outline or if you have overlooked a topic you meant to discuss. Reading for content also allows you to see whether your paper is in the right order and whether you have given adequate treatment to major points. The organization of your paper may need to be changed after this reading to be more in keeping with your outline.

You may also find places that are ambiguous or not clear to the reader. Reword these weak spots to make your paper more understandable.

This final reading should entail a look at your references to make sure they have been noted properly and that you have included all of the necessary information on your "Works Cited" page. After all, a research paper involves research—finding out what other people have said about your topic—and documenting it correctly.

MAKING THE FINAL REVISIONS

After you have finished these three readings, you not only know your paper inside and out, but you have done what is necessary for a good paper. You have learned what you have done wrong and how to go about revising it. Revising it, then, is the next step. You probably made some revisions while you read your paper; now is the time to complete your revision.

You want to be proud of the finished product. Besides producing a better paper because you have corrected your errors, you have become a better writer in the process. By learning and using these techniques, you can soon become your own best critic as you read and revise, then read and revise again.

Spend some time looking over the following rules for punctuation as you revise your paper. Then as you determine your need for additional transitions, perhaps you can find the ones you are searching for in the list of transitions on pages 112–113.

FOLLOWING RULES FOR PUNCTUATION

The rules given below are by no means all of the rules of punctuation; however, they are ones you will likely encounter in writing your research paper. After each rule, an example of its usage is given to guide you in applying it.

Using Apostrophes

1. Use an apostrophe to indicate a contraction of two words put together in a shortened form. Examples can be found on page 109.
2. Use an apostrophe to show ownership.

```
Jennifer's hat blew away.
The boys' bikes were stolen from the mall.
```

Using Brackets

1. Use brackets around the word *sic,* which means "thus," to indicate an error in the quoted sentence.

```
Shaw admitted, "Nothing can extinguish my
interest in Shakespear" [sic].
```

2. Use brackets around material that has been added to a quotation to clarify a sentence.

```
"The commissioner [Fay Vincent] ordered
George Steinbrenner to give up day-to-day
control of the New York Yankees ... "
(Matthews 116).
```

Using Colons and Semicolons

1. Use a colon to introduce a long quotation. See examples in the research papers in the appendices.
2. Use a colon to introduce a list of words.

```
The special at Jay's Barbecue includes the
following dinners: ham, pork ribs, chopped
beef, chicken, and sausage.
```

3. Use a semicolon to join two clauses of a compound sentence without a conjunction.

```
Etymology is the study of words; entomology
is the study of insects.
```

Using Commas

1. Use a comma before the conjunctions *but, and, nor,* and *or.*

   Maria asked me to go to the movie, but I
   already had plans for the evening.

2. Use a comma in a series of three or more.

   Kendra, Jim, Ellen, and Darnell have been
   friends since elementary school and now
   plan to go to the same college.

3. Use a comma to separate groups of three digits of numbers (hundreds, thousands, millions, and so on).

   Tomás paid $23,500 for his car.

4. Use a comma after an introductory phrase or clause.

   After the last hurricane in Florida, people
   evacuated quickly when the weather report
   showed another hurricane coming.

5. Use commas to set off the year in dates.

   My next doctor's appointment is August 22,
   1997, which is also my wedding anniversary.

6. Use a comma to enclose contrasting expressions.

   Congress, not the President, has the power
   to declare war.

7. Use commas to enclose appositives together with their modifiers.

   The Tasmanian devil, a ruthless marsupial,
   will attack and overcome creatures much
   larger than itself.

8. Use commas to separate lines of an address in a running text.

> ```
> Mr. Patel listed his address as 2224
> Longbeach Street, Lemoore, CA 93245.
> ```

9. Use commas to set off a direct quotation. The comma precedes the quotation marks.

> ```
> Ed Cullen said, "Steinbeck came to know
> life in the migrant camps as a journalist."
> ```

10. Use commas before and after a nonessential modifier.

> ```
> The airplane, having lost one of its en-
> gines, landed safely.
> ```

Using Contractions

1. Use contractions to indicate two words joined together in a shortened form.

> ```
> He hasn't (has not) passed the bar exam.
> ```

2. Avoid using contractions in formal writing such as a research paper.

Using Ellipsis Marks

1. Use ellipsis marks to indicate an omission in a quotation. Three dots indicate an omission; a fourth dot is added if the omission precedes or follows a period.

> ```
> In his Journal Ralph Waldo Emerson said, "I
> trust a good deal to common fame. . . . If a
> man has good corn . . . or can make better
> chairs . . . than anybody else, you will
> find a broad, hardbeaten path to his house,
> though it be in the woods."
> ```

Using Hyphens

1. Avoid ending a typed line with a hyphen *if* the sentence continues on the next page.
2. Always hyphenate between syllables and between double consonants when they come at the end of the line.

```
The doctor said he would not be wil-
ling to operate without the consent of the
family.
```

3. Do not hyphenate a word if only one letter is left at the end of the line. Begin the next line with the complete word. For example, do not hyphenate a-board, e-mancipate, or u-topia.

Using Periods

1. Use a period at the end of a statement or a command.

```
The family was disappointed that the house
did not sell.
Close the door, please, when you leave the
room.
```

Using Question Marks

1. Use a question mark after a direct question, but not after an indirect question.

```
Did you find the book I was reading?
He asked if I had found the book he was
reading.
```

Using Quotation Marks

1. Insert quotation marks around the titles of poems, essays, short stories, chapter headings, periodical articles, and songs. Examples are "A Red Red Rose" (poem); "Of Parents and Children" (essay); "Tickets, Please" (short story); "Working with More Than a File—A Document" (chapter heading); "Don't Let It End This Way" (magazine article); and "Amazing Grace" (song).

2. Use quotation marks around direct, short quotations. The quotation does not have to be dialogue.

>   Mr. Blackburn said, "Your son is the best
>   swimmer on the team."

Note: The period appears inside the quotation marks.

>   "Julius Caesar was the foremost Roman of
>   his day and perhaps the most powerful man
>   in the known world" (534).

3. Long quotations consisting of four lines or more are set off from the rest of the paper by indenting ten spaces from the left margin. The quote should be double-spaced. No quotation marks are needed because the indentation indicates the quote. The research papers in the appendices contain examples.

4. Quotation marks are added around part or all of a single line of poetry within the text. Two or three lines may also be incorporated within the text by using a slash with a space on each side (/) to separate them.

>   "I'll not weep that thou art going to leave
>   me, / There's nothing lovely here" ("I'll
>   Not Weep" 381).

5. For quotations of poetry more than three lines long, set the quotation off by indenting ten spaces from the left and double-spacing the lines.

>   Wordsworth's poem "It Is a Beauteous
>   Evening," expresses his feelings of being
>   at one with nature:
>
>   It is a beauteous evening, calm
>   and free,
>   The holy time is quiet as a Nun
>   Breathless with adoration; the
>   broad sun
>   Is sinking down in its tranquillity;
>   (309)

Using Underlining

1. Underline titles of books, plays, newspapers, long poems, films, paintings, and ships. If you use a word processor, italicize these titles instead of underlining them. Examples include *The Red Pony* (book); *Antigone* (play); *The Washington Post* (newspaper); *Paradise Lost* (long poem); *Mona Lisa* (painting); and *USS Kidd* (ship).

USING APPROPRIATE TRANSITIONS

Below is a list of transitions that you can use to make your paper read more smoothly. By no means are they all of the transitions possible. Judge each transition carefully to find the ones most suitable for your paper.

Argument or Concession
admittedly, certainly, consequently, furthermore, in fact, it is true that, nobody denies, obviously, of course, on the other hand, the fact remains, undoubtedly

Cause and Effect
accordingly, because, since, thereafter, thus, whereas

Condition
even though, if, in case, nevertheless, on condition that, therefore

Connectives
additionally, after, again, also, and, as well as, before, besides, formerly, finally, further, in addition, last, later, next, not only . . . but also, previously, since, then, too, first, second, third, and so on

Differences
although, but, even so, however, in spite of the fact that, on the contrary, on the other hand, otherwise

Similarities
as, like, likewise, resemble, similar to, just as

Emphasis
absolutely, certainly, especially, extremely, importantly, undoubtedly

Example
for example, for instance, thus, to illustrate

Place
above, alongside, below, beyond, everywhere, here, near, under

Summary
finally, in conclusion, lastly, therefore, thus, to sum up

Exercise 1: Revising

Working in small groups, read through the introduction and conclusion to a paper on cholesterol that you wrote for the exercises in Step Eight. Be sure to check for errors in spelling, punctuation, capitalization, and grammar. As a group, decide whether you are still satisfied with the content and organization of the introduction and conclusion.

Step Twelve

PREPARING THE FINAL COPY

You have now followed every step throughout this guide and have made the revisions necessary. You are ready to type your final copy, completing your assignment. This last step gives final instructions regarding the mechanics of your research paper and the order in which your instructor will probably want it turned in. By following these directions you won't hand in a less-than-perfect paper after all of your hard work.

UNDERSTANDING THE MECHANICS OF THE RESEARCH PAPER

1. Use white bond paper, 8½ by 11 inches. If you use computer paper, make sure to tear off the edges before turning in your paper.

2. Double-space your typing throughout, including quotations and the list of works cited.

3. Keep your margins consistent. Except for page numbers, leave one inch on both sides and one inch at the top and bottom. Do not justify the type if you are using a word processor.

4. Indent the first word of a paragraph five spaces from the left margin. Indent long quotations of four lines or more ten spaces from the left margin.

5. On the first page of the research paper, beginning one inch below the top of the page and flush with the left margin, type the following information:

   Your name
   Your instructor's name
   Title of the course
   Date

   Double-space again and center the title of the paper on that line. Double-space between the title and the first line of the text.

6. Do not underline your title, enclose it in quotation marks, or type it in all capital letters. Underline only those words you would underline in the text, such as the title of a book.

7. Put your last name and the page number in the top right-hand corner one-half inch from the top of the page, even on the first page. (See Figure 12.1.) Number all pages consecutively without using any punctuation and without using the letter p before the number.

Figure 12.1
Student's
name and
page number

Meriwether   1

8. Although the *MLA Handbook* does not give specific instructions for a title page, the following information is usually given and spaced accordingly:

Title of the paper, centered fifteen spaces below the top of the page

Title of course, centered twelve spaces below the title

Your instructor's name, centered two spaces below the course name

Your name, centered fifteen spaces below your instructor's name

Date, centered two spaces below your name

Ask your instructor what he or she would like you to include. A sample title page, not to scale, is shown in Figure 12.2.

9. Prepare your "Works Cited" page.
   a. Center the title "Works Cited" one inch below the top of the page. Double-space between the title and the first entry. Number the page consecutively with the other pages, as you have done on the previous pages, with your name preceding the page number.
   b. Double-space between the title and the first entry, and double-space both within and between entries.
   c. Begin each entry flush with the left margin; if the entry is more than one line, indent each following line five spaces from the left margin.
   d. Alphabetize the entries according to the author's or editor's name. If these are not given, alphabetize by the title of the work. (*Note:* Never alphabetize by the words *a, an,* or *the.*)

ORDERING THE PAGES OF YOUR PAPER

Though the order for turning in the pages of your paper may vary from instructor to instructor, the following order is usually followed:

1. Title page
2. Outline (if required)
3. Text of your paper
4. "Works Cited" page
5. Blank page

Figure 12.2
Title page

An Analysis of the Heath in Selected Works

English IV
Mrs. Nell W. Meriwether, Instructor

Mona Lisa Tyson
February 10, 1996

Now that you have finished writing your research paper, you probably feel a sense of accomplishment. This is one of many papers you will write if you plan to attend a university or college. Having learned the steps for writing a successful research paper, you should experience few difficulties in the future. This manual can help you in college as well; it follows the MLA style, which is the same format most universities use. If your instructor requires some other style, you will only need to adjust the form slightly. You have acquired the essential information about how to write a research paper, and that is what is important.

Good luck with this paper and with all of the others you will write!

Exercise 1: Preparing the Final Copy

Working in small groups, read through the sample research papers in Appendices A-C, keeping in mind all that you have learned in this book. If necessary, review any steps that may still seem difficult for you.

Appendix A

RESEARCH PAPER USING CAUSE AND EFFECT ORDER

A Picture of Destitution Yet Hope

English IV

Nell W. Meriwether

4 August 1996

Outline

Purpose: To show how Steinbeck in <u>The Grapes of Wrath</u> presents a picture of destitution so realistically that he was effective in bringing the plight of the migrants to the attention of the government and bringing about programs to help alleviate their problems

  I. Introduction

 II. Critics' judgment of Steinbeck's novel

     A. Steve Culpepper

     B. Sally Buckner

III. Themes in <u>The Grapes of Wrath</u>

     A. Social injustice

     B. Man's struggle to survive

 IV. Saga of the migrants

     A. Frustration and destitution

         1. Move to the unknown

         2. Death of Grampa

         3. Hunger of families

     B. Alienation and confusion

         1. Change in societal structure

         2. Name change to Okies

     C. Anger, hatred, and prejudice

         1. Encounters with police

         2. Treatment at Hoovervilles

         3. Tom's promise

  V. Steinbeck's protest of conditions

     A. California Growers Association's refutation

     B. Steinbeck's view of the exploitation of the land

     C. Steinbeck's attitudes toward social reform

 VI. Government recognition of migrant problems

     A. Senate Committee on Education and Labor

    B. President Roosevelt

       1. New Deal

       2. Civilian Conservation Corps

       3. Home Owners Loan Corporation

       4. Farm Security Administration

VII. Conclusion

A Picture of Destitution Yet Hope

An article entitled "She Made Her Dream Come True" in
<u>Parade Magazine</u>, May 7, 1995, tells the story of Maria Vega, the
daughter of migrant farm workers. Maria says she grew up "with
little more than a supportive family and a vision of a better
future." Maria had always wanted to be a doctor, but she never
thought that it was possible (Ryan 18).

Through a program at Boston University's medical school to
help disadvantaged youths, Maria is making her dream come true.
She says, "It's hard, but I'll do whatever it takes to get
through" (Ryan 18).

Maria as a migrant still finds it difficult because of the
constant moves her family made as she was growing up, following
one season of crops to another. Maria's plight dates back many
years. It is most poignantly made visible in John Steinbeck's
<u>The Grapes of Wrath</u>, a novel that, according to Paul McCarthy in
<u>John Steinbeck</u>, exposed mankind's "grievous faults and fail-
ures," alerting mankind to social and economic dangers and
forgotten commitments and dreams. He says that "Steinbeck's
strongest convictions and passions appear in his fundamental
belief in humanity, in his expectation that man will endure, and
that the creative forces of the human spirit will prevail"
(143).

Steinbeck wrote from experience. According to Ed Cullen in
previewing Steinbeck's <u>Working Days: The Journals of the Grapes
of Wrath</u>, "Steinbeck came to know life in the migrant camps as
a journalist. He saw firsthand an attack of grape-pickers by
strikebusters in 1936 in the town of Delano. Five thousand
starving migrant families in the flooded country around Visalia
inspired the final passages of <u>The Grapes of Wrath</u>" (121). It is
this kind of understanding and empathy that led John Steinbeck
in 1938 to write <u>The Grapes of Wrath</u> in which he realistically

Meriwether 2

presents a picture of frustration and destitution, of alienation and confusion, of anger, hatred, and prejudice against a minority of people in the United States, which helped to bring about laws protecting and/or governing migrants.

While it is evident that Steinbeck shows the terrible conditions of people in the Dust Bowl who were trying to find a better life by moving from one state to another, to measure the effect of his novel on the laws of the land is difficult to prove. On the other hand, as is the case with Maria Vega, perhaps even today his work has a lingering effect on the recognition of the migrant situation, for Maria is able to attend Boston medical school because of a program that helps prepare bright but disadvantaged students for medical school.

Steve Culpepper, in his review of The Grapes of Wrath, says the book "stands out as the monument to the time, a great big rough monolith, wide and tall and sculpted with a coarse face" (21). Then he adds further that "the book helped to focus attention on the bitter poverty and desperate helplessness of the Depression's victims, the masses of people who more or less like the Joads were forced by circumstances to leave their homes and to wander through nearly unimaginable suffering. And everywhere they went, they were loudly unwanted, abused and misunderstood" (21). Steinbeck's portrayal of these people, the Okies, was that even though they were "trapped in an unfair world, they remained sympathetic and heroic, if defeated human beings" ("Steinbeck, John Ernst," Encarta).

The publication of Steinbeck's novel created quite a stir when it was published in 1939. According to Sally Buckner, his "account of the predicament of migrant workers was taken more as social document than as fiction" (2346). Buckner adds further that the picture of oppression Steinbeck depicts is so vivid that its authenticity is questioned. She points out, as did

Cullen earlier, that Steinbeck had reason to know what the conditions were for these people. He had journeyed with the Okies
from Oklahoma to California; he had lived in a migrant camp; and
he had worked alongside the migrants (2346). Steinbeck's home
was also in California, in the Salinas Valley, so he knew firsthand what was happening when the Okies and other migrants tried
to find work in the almost feudal system of agricultural exploitation (Hart 802).

As Buckner indicates, social injustice is one of the main
themes of Steinbeck's novel. She feels that by showing the conditions the people were going through, he was trying to change
the attitudes and behavior of the people--both migrants and
economic barons (2346). She also feels that another theme in the
novel is the recognition that all men are bound together as one
and will struggle to survive. James Gray says, "Man's problem is to
learn to accept his cosmic identity, by which Steinbeck means:
to become aware of himself as an integral part of the whole
design of existence" (69). He adds, "Tom Joad said it for him
more succinctly in The Grapes of Wrath: 'Well, maybe . . . a
fella ain't got a soul of his own, but on'y a piece of a big
one'" (69).

While Steinbeck may show the plight of man as being one
of acceptance and awareness of himself, that idea is overshad-
owed by his portrayal of the injustices of society. He protests
the fact that people must leave the only homes they have ever
known, dispossessed by what some called a freak of nature, the
Dust Bowl. Then he protests the way they are treated as they
travel to the land of their dreams and the way they are horri-
bly mistreated when they get to the land.

The Okies, as they are called, did not leave their homes
on their own but were forced to leave because they had no way
of making a living. The land was devastated, cattle died, and

agriculture virtually ceased because of the Dust Bowl, which had formed because of soil erosion and a series of droughts. Sylvia Jean Cook describes them in this way: ". . . even if they are held under no legal right, the small farms they must leave are, in the consciousness of the croppers, part of themselves--the locus of their family and history. They wonder if, in abandoning them, they are not doing grave injury to the very essence of their existence" (172).

In <u>The Grapes of Wrath</u>, Steinbeck lets the tenant men describe the situation in their own way as they are being told to get off the land by the "owner men."

> . . . it's our land. We measured it and broke it up.
> We were born on it, and we got killed on it, died on
> it. Even if it's no good, it's still ours. That's what
> makes it ours--being born on it, working it, dying on
> it. That makes ownership, not a paper with numbers on
> it" (39).

They are incensed with the idea they must move, but move they must, for the bank is forcing them out. They are told the land isn't theirs simply because they have lived on it. The land belongs to the bank, the fifty-thousand-acre owners who can't be responsible for what is happening.

This begins their saga of frustration and destitution, of alienation and confusion, of anger and hatred and prejudice. Even as the tractor cuts through the dooryard, the tenant man shows his frustration: "I got to figure. We all got to figure. There's some way to stop this. It's not like lightning or earthquakes. We've got a bad thing made by man, and by God that's something we can change" (44). But the tractor just keeps on moving, and as the tenant man and his wife and children watch, the tractor bites into the house, "so that it fell sideways, crushed like a bug" (44).

Some of the farmers, like Muley Graves and Grampa Joad,
find it too much to leave the only homes they have ever known.
Muley becomes a fugitive, running from one cotton field to another evading the law, accepting his fate. He tells Tom Joad and
Jim Casey, "I was mean like a wolf. Now I'm mean like a weasel.
When you're huntin' somepin you're a hunter, an' you're
strong. . . . When you get hunted--that's different. Somepin happens to you" (60).

Grampa, though, determined he is going to stay with Muley
and fend for himself, is drugged by Ma's putting "soothin'
sirrup" in his coffee and never knows when he is put on the old
dilapidated truck. He has his own way, however; before they ever
leave Oklahoma, he has a stroke and dies. Casey sums up his
death by saying, "Your way was fixed an' Grampa didn' have no
part in it. He didn' suffer none. Not after fust thing this
mornin'. He's jus' stayin' with the lan'. He couldn't leave it"
(144).

Steinbeck's portrayal of frustration and destitution is
shown over and over as the Okies make their way to California
on U.S. Highway 66. The Joads aren't the only travelers; the
road is filled with people. Once a family with two little boys
stops for water, which is allowed begrudgingly at the truck
stop, and the father asks to buy a loaf of bread. Mae, who is
behind the counter, tells them they can only buy sandwiches, for
if they sell bread, they'll run out before the bread truck
comes. Seeing the hunger and despair on their faces, Al, who is
making sandwiches, snarls at Mae: "Goddamn it, Mae, give 'em the
loaf" (136).

Over and over that scene is repeated with the Joads and
others who are on Highway 66. Casey sees the constant moving and
tells Tom he's been watching all the cars on the road and all
of the families going west "like they was runnin' away from

soldiers" (169). He wonders out loud, "S'pose all these here folks an' ever'body--s'pose they can't get no jobs out there" (169).

The question of jobs is heightened as they stop for the night at a campground with others in the same plight. A ragged man sitting on the front porch, who has already been to California, tells Pa he's going back home to starve. He would rather starve all at once than to endure the conditions in California, where he lost his wife and two children from heart failure and starvation (185). Pa refuses to believe the ragged man's story because the handbill says there are jobs, the same handbill that thousands of others have received.

As they continue on to California, the families build their own little worlds, learning what rights must be observed. For example, "the right of privacy in the tent; the right to keep the black past hidden in the heart; the right to talk and to listen; the right to refuse help or to accept it . . ." (188). They build their worlds in the evening, and the whole structure of their social life is changed. Now they are migrant men, not tenant men, moving from one campsite to another, meeting acquaintances and talking of what has happened and what lies ahead.

A foreshadowing of what lies ahead is described by one fellow just after they reach sight of California. He says, "You gonna see in people's face how they hate you. An'--I'll tell you somepin. They hate you 'cause they're scairt. They know a hungry fella gonna get food even if he got to take it. They know that fallow lan's a sin an' somebody' gonna take it. What the hell! You never been called 'Okie' yet" (198).

Tom can't believe what he's hearing and asks what Okie means. The man replies, "Okie use' ta mean you was from Oklahoma. Now it means you're a dirty sonofabitch. Okie means you're

scum" (198). This is an eye-opener for the Joads. They don't
consider themselves scum, just people looking for a way to make
a living. Anger becomes the emotion most often seen at this
point. The Joads get their first taste of prejudice when they
next stop for the night, and a policeman orders them to move on
because they are Okies. Three hundred thousand fleeing to California, to the land flowing with milk and honey, except that it
is a land of hate and fear and intimidation and prejudice. Tom
tells Casey, "Look, this ain't no lan' of milk an' honey like
the preachers say. They's a mean thing here. The folks here is
scared of us people comin' west; an' so they got cops out
tryin' to scare us back" (243).

Steinbeck shows what it is like when the Okies reach the
land of their dreams. He shows the horrible sanitary conditions
of the migrant labor camps, called Hoovervilles after Herbert
Hoover, the president of the United States during the Great
Depression. He shows the starvation and sickness, the intimidation by the police, the constant surveillance, the beatings, the
murders, and the deaths. He describes the lush California val-
leys in this way:

> The people come with nets to fish for potatoes in the
> river, and the guards hold them back; they come in
> rattling cars to get the dumped oranges, but the kero-
> sene is sprayed . . . and in the eyes of the people
> there is failure; and in the eyes of the hungry there
> is a growing wrath. In the souls of the people the
> grapes of wrath are filling and growing heavy, growing
> heavy for the vintage (336).

The problems are immense, with thousands upon thousands of
homeless people searching for food, work, and a place to live.
It is a picture of horror, helplessness, and despair, yet
through it all, there is hope. As Tom Joad is being hunted

because he dares stand up to the authorities and fight for his
people, he knows he must leave his family. He promises Ma as he
sees her one last time that he will be a presence wherever
ordinary men and women struggle to better their lives. He says:

> I'll be all aroun' in the dark. I'll be ever'where--
> wherever you look. Wherever they's a fight so hungry
> people can eat, I'll be there. Wherever they's a cop
> beatin' up a guy, I'll be there. . . . An' when our
> folks eat the stuff they raise an' live in the houses
> they build--why I'll be there (402-3).

Steinbeck brings to light through his novel the conditions
that existed, and "[t]hough California Growers Associations
claimed that Steinbeck's picture was distorted, both congres-
sional and journalistic investigators found abundant evidence to
justify the broad thrust of his indictment" (Weisberger 443).

Steinbeck saw how the land was being exploited and how the
private industry groups, such as the Growers Association, were
reaping profits at the expense of the individual. He could not
sit still and wring his hands. Instead, he wrote the story of
the Joad family, of their misfortunes and heartaches, and in
doing so captured the attention of America to the plight of
thousands of homeless people.

According to Gray:

> He nourished within himself the attitudes toward social
> reform that were growing slowly in the national con-
> sciousness of his time. His protests, his rejections as
> well as his affirmative convictions about the hope for
> regeneration, were exactly those that have been taken
> up by leaders of opinion in a later day enabling them,
> as teachers, theorists, and legislators, to change our
> minds in the direction of greater sensibility concern-
> ing human rights. . . . He dramatized situations in

American life and espoused beliefs about the need of
room for growth in a way that helped to awaken the
conscience of his fellow Americans (70).

Though it is difficult to pinpoint the exact laws that
came about as a result of Steinbeck's exposé of the migrant
problem, in 1939 a subcommittee of the Senate Committee on Education and Labor visited California to investigate violations of
the workers' civil liberties. In his report to the Senate,
Culbert Olson testified before the Senate Committee on Education
and Labor of the horrible conditions that existed among the
migrants. He said "that the emphasis in the protection of civil
liberties should be placed upon measures designed to prevent the
occurrence of labor disputes and to decasualize agricultural
labor employment in California" (591). He stressed the fact that
migrants' rights needed to be protected, but they needed to fall
under the general social, economic, and political life of the
state in which they resided or found employment (591). Otherwise, Olson felt it would be difficult to protect their civil
liberties. Indeed, that is a difficult problem; however, the
problem was addressed then and is being addressed now to some
extent. For example, in 1983 the government passed the Migrant
Seasonal and Payroll Act, which is another step forward in addressing the situation of seasonal workers and their wages.

President Roosevelt recognized the weight of the problem
of families being dispossessed and without work by establishing
the New Deal, which set up thirty regional camps.

> "He tried to stop the erosion of the land through the
> Civilian Conservation Corps (CCC), which employed 2.5
> million young men in reforestation and flood control
> projects. . . . The Home Owners Loan Corporation lent
> money to impoverished mortgagors to guarantee the ex-
> istence of the family home . . . and the Farm Security

Meriwether 10

Administration tried to block the exodus of farmers
from their midwestern homes by providing long-term
loans at low interest and by sponsoring cooperative
buying (<u>The American Destiny</u> 65).

It is true that some of President Roosevelt's plans were
inaugurated before Steinbeck's novel, but the need for help was
made clearer through his exposé. According to Dixon Wecter,

Out of California's one hundred and fifty thousand farm
proprietors in 1939, fewer than three thousand large-
scale operators, belonging chiefly to an organization
called the Associated Farmers, employed at starvation
pay most of the two hundred thousand migrants then in
the state. This body strongly resented the unionization
of agricultural labor . . . and tension mounted until
the exigencies of war industry raised wages and en-
forced a truce (175).

One would not like to think that the war was a cure for
Steinbeck's migrants, but it did give everybody something to do
and something to work for together.

Steinbeck's portrayal of the migrant situation--frustra-
tion, destitution, alienation, confusion, anger, hatred, and
prejudice--was a realistic portrayal of life in the late 1930s.
Though some may disagree, Joseph R. Millichap characterizes
Steinbeck in this way: "No American writer has better exposed
the dark underside of the American Dream nor better traced the
lineament of the American Nightmare--and few have so successfully celebrated the great hope which underlies the belief in
human potential" (178). Even today man still hears the sounds of
Steinbeck's novel drumming on the heartstrings of society with
the same beat--to awaken all men to the plight of the homeless,
the migrants, and to respond to their needs.

Meriwether 11

Works Cited

The American Destiny. Ed. Henry Steele Commager. Vol. 14. Oak-
     land, ME: Danbury P, 1976.

Buckner, Sally. "The Grapes of Wrath." Masterplots. Ed. Frank N.
     Magill. Vol. 4. Englewood Cliffs, NJ: Salem, 1976.

Cook, Sylvia Jean. From Tobacco Road to Route 66. Chapel Hill:
     U. of North Carolina P, 1976.

Cullen, Ed. "Steinbeck Journal: Grapes of Wrath Between the
     Lines." Sunday Advocate [Baton Rouge] 7 July 1989: 21.

Culpepper, Steve. "The Grapes of Wrath Remains Monument to Great
     Depression." Sunday Advocate [Baton Rouge] 2 July 1989: 29.

Gray, James. American Writers: A Collection of Literary Biogra-
     phies. Ed. Leonard Unger. Vol. IV. New York: Scribners,
     1971.

Hart, James D. "Steinbeck, John." The Oxford Companion to Ameri-
     can Literature. New York: Oxford UP, 1965.

McCarthy, Paul. John Steinbeck. New York: Ungar, 1980.

Millichap, Joseph R. Steinbeck and Film. New York: Ungar, 1983.

Olson, Culbert L. "Migratory Labor and Civil Liberties."
     Encyclopaedia Britannica 1986 ed.

Ryan, Michael. "She Made Her Dream Come True." Parade Magazine 7
     May 1995: 18.

"Steinbeck, John Ernst." Encarta. Microsoft Corp. America
     Online. 15 June 1995.

Steinbeck, John. The Grapes of Wrath. 1939. Pleasantville, New
     York: Reader's Digest, 1991.

Wecter, Dixon. The Age of the Great Depression. New York:
     Macmillan, 1948.

Weisberger, Bernard A. Afterword. The Grapes of Wrath. By John
     Steinbeck. Pleasantville, New York: Reader's Digest, 1991.

Appendix B

RESEARCH PAPER USING COMPARISON/CONTRAST ORDER

Tyson 1

Mona Lisa Tyson

Nell W. Meriwether, Instructor

English IV

10 February 1996

                  An Analysis of the Heath in Selected Works

          Each geographical region around the world, whether small

or large, country or continent, has a portion of land within its

boundaries that overpowers and dominates all others. For ex-

ample, the dry deserts of Africa, the swamplands of Louisiana,

and the extreme conditions of Siberia in Russia. These vast and

distinctive areas possess individual characteristics that enable

each to overwhelm its inhabitants, surrounding lands, and

oftentimes nature itself.

          The previous examples give an idea of the role that the

heath plays in <u>Wuthering Heights</u>, <u>King Lear</u>, and <u>The Return of</u>

<u>the Native</u>. Harold Bloom quotes Hardy, saying:

               The face of the heath by its mere complexion added half

               an hour to evening; it could in like manner retard the

               dawn, sudden noon, anticipate the frowning of storms

               scarcely generated, and intensify the opacity of a

               moonless midnight to a cause of shaking and dread

               (*Views* 22).

According to Thomas Hardy, author of <u>The Return of the Native</u>,

the heath is a barren land, occupying space as far as the eye

can see, making its inhabitants, who look out upon it during the

darkest hours of night, feel a sense of being trapped, never to

escape the ongoing obstacle, and also keeping their minds con-

stantly wondering about the world beyond (56).

          Not only Hardy, but also Emily Brontë and William

Shakespeare have their own thoughts about the heath. Even though

their styles and interpretations differ slightly, it is evident

through the selected works that Hardy, Brontë, and Shakespeare
share the same feeling. They emphasize the effect the heath has
on the lives of their characters by directly associating it with
the characters and their surrounding conditions.

Admittedly, an opposite point of view can be supported
showing that Brontë, Shakespeare, and Hardy do not use the heath
symbolically nor do they directly relate it to the characters
and their daily situations. This opinion can indeed be argued;
however, there is more substantial evidence and indication in
their works to convincingly show the effective use of the heath.

Wuthering Heights, a novel written by Emily Brontë, is a
passionate story of unkindled love, hatred, strife, and revenge.
What seems to be an endless conflict is basically centered
around the Earnshaws and the Lintons, two families who are proprietors of separate plots of land, and Heathcliff, an orphan
whose character further increases the intensity of the conflict.
Wuthering Heights and Thrushcross Grange are the plots of land
previously mentioned, which are significantly divided by the
heath. This open tract of wasteland, which Brontë occasionally
refers to as the moors, presents itself not only as a natural
obstacle to those who travel through it, but also as a way of
looking at Heathcliff's inner being.

The heath definitely symbolizes barrenness and wildness in
Wuthering Heights. Tom Winnifrith agrees that the heath is like
a harsh landscape that is like barren moors (60). This stretch
of "untamed" land is portrayed as a mighty hindrance and burden
to those who live and travel upon it. In Wuthering Heights, Mr.
Lockwood says, "Yesterday afternoon set in misty and cold. I had
half a mind to spend it by the fire, instead of wading through
the heath and mud to Wuthering Heights" (6). This obviously
shows that the heath is not a desirable place to be nor to pass
through due to unfavorable conditions.

The characters of <u>Wuthering Heights</u> are essential elements when considering the heath and its dominant characteristics. The heath causes an inevitable effect on the characters, because there is such a close relationship between them. The inhabitants of such an overbearing land as the heath are not able to avoid some kind of physical or mental contact with it. In the novel, Heathcliff is more closely related to the heath than any other character. Winnifrith states, ". . . <u>Wuthering Heights</u> is set in a wild landscape, and it is part of Heathcliff's attraction that he is associated with the landscape and with Wuthering Heights" (65). Heathcliff has a certain sense of oneness with the heath. Even his name is linked to the heath. In her introduction to the second edition of <u>Wuthering Heights</u>, Brontë gives a shocking hint concerning the origins of Heathcliff's name. Winnifrith quotes her as saying:

> Most readers will think of a heath as an arid waste as in <u>King Lear</u>, and there are plenty of barren wastes on the moors near Wuthering Heights and in Heathcliff's heart. But there is also a small flower named a heath, and it is to this that links the mighty and rugged cliff that stands for <u>Wuthering Heights</u> (67).

Critics have always had something to say about <u>Wuthering Heights</u>, whether good or bad. The following critical reviews by Hobart, Garrod, and Schorer are accredited to <u>Nineteenth-Century Literary Criticism</u> and show the critics' impression of the heath. Hobart acknowledges <u>Wuthering Heights</u> as:

> . . . a picture of fierce and strong human nature, utterly untutored and untamed, left to run wild in the gloomy loneliness of a farm on the northern moors (67).

Garrod comments:

> Out of the defects, <u>Wuthering Heights</u> is redeemed, first, by its strong instinct for a living scene--

nowhere else, perhaps save in <u>Lear</u>, are the scene and
the actors to the same degree a single tragical effect
(78).

Garrod continues:

The very title "Wuthering Heights" is a stroke of in-
spiration. Heathcliff has just one name, no other, as
though he were a piece of the moorland--"an arid wilderness" . . . (78).

Finally, Mark Schorer remarks in the same criticism, "Human
conditions are like the activities of the landscape; faces, too,
are like landscapes in <u>Wuthering Heights</u>" (91). These critics,
in expounding upon the relationship between the heath and the
characters of the novel, show the strong impact of the heath
upon the tragic events that occur.

Another literary work already alluded to that stresses the
effect of the heath on the characters is <u>King Lear</u>, one of
Shakespeare's greatest plays. It is a powerful tragedy about an
aged king who decides to divide his kingdom among his three
daughters, giving the largest share to the one who can prove she
loves him most. The youngest and favorite daughter refuses her
father's request because she can see the deceit in her two older
sisters in their professions of love. King Lear is outraged, and
he banishes her from his kingdom, giving the land to the two
remaining daughters. Soon after, Lear's daughters become un-
grateful and strip him of everything he owns, which then leads
to the king's insanity. When King Lear goes out on the heath
amidst a terrible storm, he is at a breaking point in his life.
It is the climax of the story as he realizes the foolishness of
his actions. Later he dies of a broken heart.

In <u>King Lear</u>, the heath again symbolizes an "arid" and
desolate land and is often compared with the heath in <u>Wuthering</u>

<u>Heights</u>, but there is an underlying purpose in Shakespeare's heath. Not only is it the place where he pours his heart out as he realizes the futility of his actions, it is also a comforter to Lear as he confesses his mistakes. Accompanied by his Fool in the storm, he gains compassion and understanding from his surroundings even though he is weakened and at the point of insanity.

In <u>Essentials of English Literature</u>, Bernard Grebanier states, "The elements are now raging. Amidst sheets of lightning, volleys of thunder, and cascades of rain, Lear wanders on the heath in the company of his Fool" (120). Sylvia Goulding affirms that what happened upon the heath during that fierce storm was a turning point in King Lear's life; his insanity and rage cause him to go out in such a storm and relieve his mind of his burdens (19).

In Act Three, Scene Four, Lear is truly at his lowest level in life. It is at this moment on the heath that he reaches his catharsis, meaning that the foolishness of his actions are revealed to him. Russell Fraser, in the introduction to <u>The Tragedy of King Lear</u>, writes, "It is also on the heath that Lear is made pregnant to pity" (23). This is an indication of the severity of his sorrow and distress. It is clear then that King Lear reaches the climax of his desperate situation on the heath with Edgar and his Fool (Foster 1164). Even though the luxuries of kingship are taken from him, it is on the heath that Lear touches his true inner self and the real experiences of the people and the world around him that he could not acquire among the glory and power of being a king.

Another literary work, <u>The Return of the Native</u> by Thomas Hardy, also uses the heath in such proportions that it achieves nearly anthropomorphic proportions, the first chapter's being

devoted almost entirely to a discussion of the heath. The two
opposing forces in the novel are Egdon Heath, a vast tract of
wasteland, and Eustacia Vye, a young woman struggling against
the heath in vain. All other actions in the story seem to be
concentrated around these two forces.

The plot basically consists of a small group of people who
are trying to solve major conflicts among themselves but are not
too successful, because they are faced with the presence and
dominating personality of the heath each day of their lives.
Egdon Heath presents itself as a no-way-out situation. Nothing
leaves the realms of Egdon Heath.

Thomas Hardy was born almost on Egdon Heath--which he made
immortal--in Dorset, near Dorchester. Egdon Heath is a justifi-
able portrayal of his homeland at Higher Bockhampton on the edge
of Puddleton Heath. Because of Hardy's close association with
the heath, it explains why Egdon Heath is such a dominating
force in the novel.

Though Hardy wrote a number of novels, <u>The Return of the
Native</u> is the only one that precisely links the land with the
plot throughout the entire book. Woodcock in the introduction to
<u>The Return of the Native</u> states:

> When Hardy describes the face of the Heath, with its
> seasonal moods and diurnal changes, . . . he is working
> from memory, and it is not surprising that on these
> occasions he slips into the manner of a rural essayist
> rather than a writer of fiction (15).

Hardy's experiences with the heath as a child give him a cutting
edge when he writes his novels.

Hardy describes the heath as a vast stretch of wild land
with no boundaries. It is like the floor of a tent made up of
an empty stretch of clouds that block the sky (53). This allows

the mind to form a mental picture of how massive and coarse the heath really is. It is illustrated as a living landscape that humans must be bound to if they are to survive. Those who lack in the kind of determination to survive tend to struggle with the land, which in the end leads to failure in life or death. The heath is an "untameable" stretch of land that regards civilization as its enemy, rejects vegetation on its soil, and wears the natural and unchanged look as it did when it was first formed (56). Hardy further adds, "The sea changed, the fields changed, the rivers, the villages, and the people changed, yet Egdon remained" (56). This gives a definite account of the heath's uniform structure and appearance throughout time. Hardy explains an overall atmospheric view of the heath when he says:

> It could be best felt when it could not clearly be
> seen, its complete effect and explanation lying in this
> and the succeeding hours before the next dawn. Then,
> and only then, did it tell its true tale (53).

In The Return of the Native, Egdon Heath represents more than just the root of the inhabitants' sufferings, though it is thought to be the basis of their troubles. Wester says, "The Heath acts as more than the setting; it assumes a part as a major character" (1894), while Gregor feels that Egdon Heath can be introduced as the chief character of the novel (69). Gregor argues that though Hardy explains the role distinction of the heath between "land" and "character" in the beginning chapters of the novel, there is still difficulty in understanding how the heath makes such a transition. He declares:

> The ruling passions of the protagonists in The Return
> of the Native, and the awesome powers of the Heath need
> to be treated as forces of like nature--the Heath mani-
> festing the same impulses as do the fictional
> characters (95).

This interpretation by Gregor expounds on the fact that Egdon Heath is a major character in the novel.

The heath has another significant role. It is the place where Mrs. Yeobright, Eustacia, and Wildeve die. These deaths confirm the belief that the heath is a firm enemy, and those who fight against it will eventually die.

The influences of Egdon Heath are gripping and long lasting. Six main characters in The Return of the Native acquire a characteristic from the heath. Clym, Mrs. Yeobright, and Diggory Venn share its appearance of separateness. A quality of stamina is seen in Clym, Thomasin, and Venn. Finally, Eustacia and Wildeve share beginning liveliness and fairness to others (Bloom Views 55). Woodcock writes, "It [the novel] is set in Egdon Heath whose lowering 'titanic' presence dominates the men and women who live on it . . ." (Blurb, Return). These statements indicate that Egdon Heath controlled the lives of the inhabit-ants and reveal the influential power of such a barren wasteland.

Out on the heath, Mrs. Yeobright notices Clym, her son, at work and describes his appearance as being "not more distin-guishable from the scene around him than the green caterpillar from the leaf it feeds on" (Bloom Interpretations 81). Her statement suggests that the inhabitants of the heath blend to-gether. Basically, the identifiable features and characteristics of a person are consumed by the heath, and his individuality is drained and absorbed into the land. Later she says, "He [Clym] appeared as a mere parasite of the Heath . . . having no knowl-edge of anything in the world but fern, furze, heath, liches, and moss" (Bloom Interpretations 81). This establishes a summary of how the heath constantly preys upon the people and how there is not an escape from the overwhelming and unseen boundaries that confine the inhabitants of their fate.

Tyson   9

Opinions, however, are usually divided when it comes to critiquing <u>The Return of the Native</u> regarding the heath. Some critics have a difficult time figuring out which point to emphasize or which side to take; however, reviews by Gregor, Weston, Scott-James, and Welton are concise and straight to the point. According to Gregor:

> When the reader comes to reflect upon his experience of reading <u>The Return of the Native</u>, he is left, I think, with the distinct impression that the dramatic life of the novel is vividly present in the first book, which is dominated by Egdon Heath . . . (69).

Wester points out in her criticism that "the Heath becomes a symbol of permanence" (1894). Scott-James notes:

> Hardy's magnificent beginning of <u>The Return of the Native</u>, showing in the description of Egdon Heath what sort of place it is in which the persons are to suffer, creates an impression of nature more somber than we have had before, indeed a nature that appears to share the suffering of man (7).

Finally, Welton, in <u>Great Writers of the English Language</u>, writes, "The wilderness of Egdon Heath . . . provides a somber, brooding backdrop for the passionate love stories played out in this gripping tale" (74). She concludes, "The monotonous way of life for the people of the Heath and the slow pace at which the novel progresses carries with it a sense of timelessness and inevitability" (74). It is clear, then, from critics as well as from simply reading the novel, that the heath is a viable force in the lives of the characters and in what happens to them.

It is also obvious, after extensive research, that the characters and their circumstances are symbolically and directly affected by the heath in <u>Wuthering Heights</u>, <u>King Lear</u>, and <u>The</u>

<u>Return of the Native</u>. The heath proves itself to be an invin-
cible foe against anyone or anything that steps into its mighty
walls. It is even personified as possessing human qualities,
achieving anthropomorphic proportions. Bloom best describes the
heath in all three works as being "slighted, enduring, obscure,
obsolete, and superseded by none" (<u>Interpretations</u> 122). After
close analysis, it is evident that the heath, that massive
stretch of wild and desolate land, possesses power and strength
beyond the imagination.

Tyson 11

Works Cited

Abbey, Cherie D. and Janet Mullane, eds. <u>Nineteenth-Century</u>
    <u>Literary Criticism</u>. Vol. 16. Detroit: Gale, 1987.

Bloom, Harold, ed. <u>Modern Critical Views: Thomas Hardy</u>. New
    York: Chelsea, 1987.

---. <u>Modern Critical Interpretations: Thomas Hardy's Return of</u>
    <u>the Native</u>. New York: Chelsea, 1987.

Brontë, Emily. <u>Wuthering Heights</u>. New York: Bantam, 1981.

Foster, Edward E. "King Lear." <u>1300 Critical Evaluations of</u>
    <u>Selected Novels</u>. Ed. Frank N. Magill. Vol. 2. Englewood
    Cliffs, NJ: Salem P, 1978.

Fraser, Russell. Introduction. <u>The Tragedy of King Lear</u>. By
    William Shakespeare. New York: Penguin, 1987, 23.

Goulding, Sylvia and Jude Welton, eds. <u>Great Writers of the</u>
    <u>English Language</u>. New York: Marshall Cavendish, 1989.

Grebanier, Bernard D. N., <u>Essentials of English Literature</u>. Vol.
    1. New York: Barron's, 1959.

Gregor, Ian. "Landscapes with Figures." <u>Modern Critical Inter-</u>
    <u>pretations: Thomas Hardy's Return of the Native</u>. New York:
    Chelsea, 1987.

Hardy, Thomas. <u>The Return of the Native</u>. New York: Penguin,
    1978.

Scott-James, R. A. "Thomas Hardy: The Novels and the Dynasts."
    <u>British Writers</u>. Ed. Ian Scott-Kilbert. Vol. 6. New York:
    Scribner's, 1983.

Shakespeare, William. <u>The Tragedy of King Lear</u>. New York: Pen-
    guin, 1987.

Wester, Janet. "The Return of the Native." <u>1300 Critical Evalua-</u>
    <u>tions of Selected Novels and Plays</u>. Ed. Frank N. Magill.
    Vol. 3. Englewood Cliffs, N.J.: Salem P, 1978.

Winnifrith, Tom. "Emily Brontë." <u>Dictionary of Literary Biogra-</u>
     <u>phy</u>. Eds. Ira B. Nadel and William E. Fredeman. Vol. 21.
     Detroit: Gale, 1983.
Woodcock, George. Introduction. <u>The Return of the Native</u>. By
     Thomas Hardy. New York: Penguin, 1978.

Appendix C

RESEARCH PAPER USING PARTICULAR TO GENERAL ORDER AND ENDNOTES

ENDNOTES: ANOTHER FORM OF REFERENCING

For many years, students were advised to use a form of referencing in which the Latin terms *ibid., op. cit.,* and *loc. cit.* were used for subsequent references after the first reference was made. The latest edition of the *MLA Handbook* discourages its use, simply advising that these abbreviations are not to be used.

Another form of referencing, endnotes, is often used instead of parenthetical notation. The references are numbered consecutively, with an abbreviated form used for the second referencing. The reader then finds the source at the end of the paper instead of throughout the paper. Because this form is also widely used, directions for its use are included in this section. See the sample paper that follows for examples.

Note Numbers

1. Number the references consecutively throughout the paper.
2. Raise the number slightly above the line, after the punctuation.
3. Place the number after the sentence or quoted material.

Form for the Endnote Page

1. The endnote page immediately follows the text of the research paper, with the title "Notes" centered one inch from the top of the page.
2. Indent five spaces, set the reference number slightly above the line, and begin the first line of the entry.
3. Subsequent lines of the entry are flush to the left margin.
4. Begin with the author's or editor's name, first name first, followed by a comma.
5. The title of the work follows the name, with no punctuation after it.
6. Next include the publication information *in parentheses,* with no punctuation following it.
7. The page number appears last, followed by a period.

If you are using the endnotes page, remember to include enough information so that the work can be identified. See the sample paper for examples.

"Bibliography" Page

The Bibliography page is needed to provide source information when endnotes are used for referencing.

1. This page comes after the endnotes page.
2. All entries appear in alphabetical order.
3. The author's or editor's last name appears first, then first name, with a period following it. This helps you to alphabetize the entries.
4. The title of the work comes next, followed by a period.
5. The publication data (not in parentheses), followed by a period, appears after the title.
6. Page numbers are not included unless you are citing a periodical.
7. Entries begin at the left-hand margin with the second and third lines indented five spaces (or one-half inch). All entries are double-spaced.

In Step Ten, Compiling the "Works Cited" Page, information was given concerning the different sources you might use. The information is essentially the same for the "Bibliography" page. Use the guidelines from Step Ten to help you cite your sources.

Milton's Satan and the Byronic Hero

English IV

Sara Elizabeth Popham
5 December 1995

Outline

Purpose: To show that Byron's heroes are based on Milton's Satan because Byron was attempting to clearly restate the beliefs that he felt Milton said only vaguely in <u>Paradise Lost</u>.

Introduction

   I. Con viewpoint

      A. Byron's personal beliefs

      B. Byron's characters' beliefs

  II. Similarities in Byron's Lucifer and Milton's Satan

      A. Ways they are similar

      B. Byron's words versus Byron's true feelings

III. Speeches

      A. <u>Paradise Lost</u>

      B. <u>Cain</u>

  IV. Popular beliefs

      A. <u>Paradise Lost</u>

      B. Romantic Era

   V. Outcasts of society

      A. <u>Paradise Lost</u>

      B. <u>Childe Harold</u>

      C. <u>Cain</u>

  VI. Haunted heroes (past wrongs)

      A. <u>Paradise Lost</u>

      B. <u>Cain</u>

      C. <u>Manfred</u>

VII. Protest establishment

      A. <u>Paradise Lost</u>

      B. Ann Radcliffe

      C. <u>Cain</u>

      D. <u>Childe Harold</u>

      E. <u>Don Juan</u>

Conclusion

Milton's Satan and the Byronic Hero

John Milton wrote <u>Paradise Lost</u> during a time in which strict Puritanism and severe religious practices were the law in England. Absolute reverence and fear of God were the most prized virtues. Milton, a Puritan, wrote an epic that was a retelling of the biblical story of man's expulsion from the paradise of Eden. Through the ages, however, people have seen Milton's <u>Paradise Lost</u> in a new and different light. For many reasons, some believe that it was Satan, and not God or man, that Milton intended to be the hero of <u>Paradise Lost</u>.

Milton never states that Satan is the hero; in fact, he denounces Satan at every available opportunity in his work. However, there are certain aspects of the story that tell a different side. For instance, while God seems to play a small role, Satan is given long speeches, and his statements are made up of the strongest, most effective language. No point he makes is ever disproved. Also, Satan seems to support the Puritan cause, while God seems to represent the tyrant king who has no real right to rule. Satan is the one who opposes God, claiming in dramatic, reasonable tones why he should be deposed. Shelley, in his "Defense of Poetry," says that Satan is actually more humane than God because when God punished Adam, it seems to be out of malicious sadism rather than out of any real wish to teach Adam repentance.[1]

In fact, it is the Romantic interpretation of Milton's Satan by poets like Shelley, Coleridge, and Blake that really seem to make a hero out of Satan.[2] "Nothing can exceed the energy and magnificence of the character of Satan as expressed in <u>Paradise Lost</u>," Shelley says.[3] Blake says that Milton is "of the devil's party without knowing it," suggesting that Milton intends for Satan to be his hero, and even puts part of himself

into his character.[4] Shelley even uses Milton's Satan as a basis
for his own hero. Prometheus, in "Prometheus Unbound," says,
"The only imaginary being resembling in any degree Prometheus is
Satan."[5]

George Gordon, Lord Byron, is another Romantic poet who is
said to have "slapped British prudery in the face."[6] His poems
are full of revolutionary heroes and protests against convention
and conservatives. Byron despises poems that praise "sensibility
and sympathy," and he declares "allegiance" to Milton.[7] In many
ways his heroes closely resemble Milton's Satan and support his
values. While Milton is writing for Puritans and has to defend
God and make Him triumphant, Byron does not have to, something
that must have pleased him--and perhaps Shelley and Blake as
well. He sees this character of Romantic rebellions possessing
"courage never to submit or yield"[8] and never allows him to be
defeated in his own stories. He takes up Milton's cause in a
way that Milton never could. Byron bases his heroes on Milton's
Satan because he is trying to restate clearly the beliefs that
he thinks Milton has said only vaguely in Paradise Lost.

Contrarily, some argue that Byron was merely stating the
beliefs of any Romantic poet. Thorslev in The Byronic Hero says,
"the 'aggressive and inventive' heroes are the basis for Romantic
self-reliance."[9] Blake praises "the imaginative artist as the
true hero."[10] Others claim that Byron did not believe as his
characters did. Byron himself states this of his characters
Lucifer and Cain in Cain. He claims that he does not agree with
them, that he is merely giving them the appropriate attitudes
for their parts. However, there are many points to challenge
this.

To see the influence of Milton on Byron, the similarities
between Milton's Satan and Byron's Lucifer must be examined.

Popham 3

Both of them have powerful and convincing speeches condemning
God for his unfair practices. They do so with patient reason and
quite plausible arguments. When asked by one of the fallen an-
gels if he would return to Heaven if God decided to forgive
him, Milton's Satan replies that "It is better to reign in Hell,
than serve in Heaven."[11] When confronted with the charge that he
brings evil to the world, Byron's Lucifer says:

> Evil and good are things in their own essence,
>
> And not made good or evil by the Giver;
>
> But if He gives you good--so call him;
>
> If evil springs from him, do not name it mine.[12]

In these examples, not only the distinct similarities
between the two characters are seen, but also the sense repre-
sented by both. Byron says he does not believe as his characters
believe, but in no place in the story does Byron ever disprove,
or even dispute, their point of view. God appears to be exactly
what Lucifer implies he is--"a gloomy tyrant who denies man
knowledge and imposes submission by ignorance."[13] The "good"
people in the story are kind to each other, but they are totally submissive to God and lack any character or individuality.
When confronted by God for killing his brother, Cain claims that
he himself is nothing more than "such as thou [God] madst him;
and seeks nothing/Which must be won by kneeling. . . ."[14] This
shows how much more interesting and complex a character Cain is
than any of his "good" family. Byron seems only to demonstrate
Cain's bravery and independence in daring to challenge God and
to desire nothing that can be acquired only by being subservi-
ent. For all that Byron denies, he shares his heroes' beliefs in
<u>Cain</u>, if not stated, at least unconsciously.

Certainly, this brings up one of the major similarities
between the heroes of Byron and Milton's Satan. Even while Byron

denies his allegiance to them, Satan and the Byronic heroes are
constantly giving convincing, powerful speeches that prove the
rightness of their stand beyond doubt, and no event in the story
seems to disprove what they say. Blake says in his <u>Milton</u> that
Milton's Spectre is Satan and that "Milton acknowledges the
validity of Reason, his Spectre. Once Milton is united with his
Spectre, he can preach effectively to the public."[15] Steadman in
<u>Milton and the Paradoxes of Renaissance Heroism</u>, states that
"Milton's allegations clash with his demonstrations."[16] And, so
it appears, do Byron's.

    One prime example of the way in which Byron's heroes and
Milton's Satan seem to get the reader on the side of their
characters is the manner in which their characters echo the
beliefs of the people of that time. In <u>Paradise Lost</u>, Satan is
a supporter of the Puritan cause. As the Puritans did with
Charles I, Satan attempts to overthrow what he believes to be a
tyrant king. Another example is the way in which Satan refers to
a belief that, in Milton's time, was "dear to men."[17] When Satan
enters Hell for the first time, he cries:

      Hail horrors, hail

      Infernal world, and thou profoundest Hell

      Receive thy new Possessor; One who brings

      A mind not to be chang'd by Place or Time.

      The mind is its own place, and in itself

      Can make a Heav'n of Hell, a Hell of Heav'n.[18]

This was the popular belief of Milton's time--that it was
the set of a person's own mind that determined whether he was
happy or unhappy, not a place or time.[19]

    Similarly, this technique appears again in Byron's works.
All of Byron's heroes, no matter what evil they have done, stand
as examples of the popular Romantic hero--a fiercely independent, rebellious individual who defies authority and who sets

out on his own. In fact, the Byronic hero is a reminder of Milton's Satan in that both are wanderers, loners, and outcasts of society. Satan, of course, is an outcast of Heaven. Even the title <u>Paradise Lost</u> seems to be a woeful reminder that man is not the only one who lost paradise.

Thorslev says that Byron's Childe Harold "has an echo" of <u>Paradise Lost</u>'s Satan.[20] Childe Harold is considered the "first important Byronic hero" and the "prototype for all the rest."[21] Of <u>Childe Harold I</u> and <u>II</u>, Thorslev further adds that the hero was no "final consistency of character or outlook," but that in <u>Childe Harold III</u> and <u>IV</u>, he has "rejected order in preference of skepticism, reason, and freedom."[22] Childe Harold is the "wandering outlaw of his own dark mind."[23] The society in which he lives exiles him, so he in turn rejects them to live a life of "proud solitude."[24] Cain is an exile, too, turned away by his own people to be a reject of humanity.

Cain, of course, is rejected because of his sin, which is deemed by God to be unforgivable--the jealous murder of his brother. This is an example of another similarity between Milton's Satan and the Byronic hero--both are haunted by their past wrongs. The beauty of this is that neither Satan nor Byron's heroes will admit that they have committed a wrong. Perhaps this is because neither Milton nor Byron really feel they have. Satan attempts to overthrow God, and as a result, is condemned forever to exile in Hell. Certainly, his deed will haunt him forever simply because he can never return to paradise.

In a similar way, Cain will always be haunted by his deed because he must spend the rest of his life in exile from society. Both Satan and Cain, however, accept their punishment proudly, as though it were an honor to be rejected by a society that they both so desperately despise. The bottom line is that neither Satan nor Cain is sorry.

Manfred is another Byronic hero who is haunted by a past deed. Like a "typical Byronic hero," he is "haunted by a remorse for some dark crime."[25] The storyline hints that he may have committed incest with his sister, an interesting charge because Byron himself was accused of incest with his half-sister, Augusta Leigh.[26] Manfred searches for his sister who has run away, and when he finally finds her, he dies upon seeing her. Manfred is a soul tortured by his own deed, and yet he refuses to repent. He dies rejecting both the demons of Hell and the Christian religion.

This is an example of the way in which both Milton's Satan and Byron's heroes reject authority and the establishment. The Satan of Paradise Lost scorns the whole idea of regulated, ordered authority in which the ruler has no justified right to rule. He says that he "reigns" in Hell, but this seems to be only because he has earned the position by taking the lead in the rebellion. Where Byron's heroes are concerned, this seems to still hold true. The people in Byron's works "submit" to his heroes because "they recognize leadership, even in one who is for independence and individual freedom."[27]

Similarly, Ann Radcliffe, a Romantic novelist, displays her views of the establishment in The Italian. Her Romantic hero would rather live in his own tortured world than "accept a world where cause and effect are providentially and naturally ordered."[28] This Romantic interpretation is one that Byron shares. He blames the establishment and corrupt rulers for the sins of his heroes. "The typical political situation [of the Byronic work] is that the evils of despotism produce criminals or outlaws but that crime, though not condoned, is less wicked, less hypocritical, than the society which produces it."[30]

Certainly, this holds true for Byron's <u>Cain</u>. The story seems to imply that Cain was "forced into murder by opposition to God" and that because "evil procures evil," God is really at fault for Cain's weaknesses, as is the society that worships him.[31] It is also true of Don Juan, a "hero who belongs to no social order" who would "castigate the British 'establishment' from a personal position of exile."[32] In <u>The Vision of Judgment</u>, Byron's hero cries, "God save the king!" The passages after that statement suggest that God had better save the king because the king is a sinner who needs saving. In <u>Childe Harold</u>, the Byronic hero claims, "I am as a weed, flung from a rock."[33] This seems to suggest that Harold is "a victim of circumstances rather than the master of his fate."[34] So, Milton seems to imply, is Satan.

As previously mentioned, Shelley says that his Prometheus most closely resembles Milton's Satan. Thorslev also says that Shelley's Prometheus is a Byronic hero because he is "an individual, skeptic, and rebel."[35] Milton's Satan is considered, especially in the Romantic Age, to be the hero of <u>Paradise Lost</u>. Many poets and writers have modeled their heroes on the idea of an independent, rebellious, wandering character who scorns authority and lives his life away from society. Byron's heroes go far beyond the classical model of a Romantic hero. Because of the era in which he lived, Milton was not able to clearly air his views on what a hero should be, or so Byron thought. During the rebellious Romantic Age, Milton's Satanic hero "came into style." In view of their similar attitudes, values, and actions, it is clear that Byron based his heroes, not just on a common Romantic theme, but on Milton's Satanic hero in particular, attempting to restate the beliefs that he felt Milton had said only vaguely in <u>Paradise Lost</u>.

Byron believed that "a poet's first moral duty is to the truth."[36] More than anything, Byron wanted to state the truth

about life and society. He believed that Milton knew the truth,
and he wanted everyone through his own works to be sure of that
truth.

Notes

[1]Peter L. Thorslev, Jr., <u>The Byronic Hero</u> (U.S.A.: Lund P, 1962) 111.

[2]Thorslev, 109.

[3]Thorslev, 111

[4]"Milton," <u>Encyclopedia Britannica</u>, 1988 ed.

[5]Thorslev, 111.

[6]Julian Hill, <u>Great English Poets</u> (London: E. Grant Richards, 1907) 233.

[7]"English Literature," <u>Encyclopedia Britannica</u>, 1988 ed.

[8]Thorslev, 178.

[9]Thorslev, 110.

[10]"English Literature," <u>Encyclopedia Britannica</u>.

[11]John Milton, <u>Paradise Lost</u> (New York: Odyssey P, 1935) 18.

[12]Malcolm Kelsall, "George Gordon, Lord Byron, *Cain*," <u>British Writers</u>, ed. Ian Scott-Kilbert, Vol. IV (New York: Scribner's, 1981) 181.

[13]Kelsall, 181.

[14]Kelsall, 181.

[15]Joseph Natoli, "William Blake," <u>Critical Survey of Poetry</u>, Vol. IV. (Englewood Cliffs, NJ: Salem P, 1982) 218.

[16]John M. Steadman, <u>Milton and the Paradoxes of Renaissance Heroism</u> (Baton Rouge, LA: L.S.U.P., 1987) 113.

[17]Milton, 17.

[18]Milton, 17.

[19]Milton, 17.

[20]Thorslev, 131.

[21]Thorslev, 128.

[22]Thorslev, 122.

[23]Kelsall, 175.

[24]Kelsall, 176.

[25]Kelsall, 179.

[26]"Byron," _Encyclopedia Britannica_, 1988 ed.

[27]Kelsall, 175.

[28]E. B. Murray, _Anne Radcliffe_ (New York: Twayne, 1972) 158.

[29]Murray, 158.

[30]Murray, 158.

[31]Kelsall, 181.

[32]Kelsall, 171.

[33]Kelsall, 176.

[34]Kelsall, 176.

[35]Thorslev, 124.

[36]Kelsall, 189.

Bibliography

"Byron." <u>Encyclopedia Britannica</u>. 1988 ed.

"English Literature." <u>Encyclopedia Britannica</u>. 1988 ed.

Hill, Julian. <u>Great English Poets</u>. London: E. Grant Richards, 1907.

Kelsall, Malcolm. "Gordon, George, Lord Byron. <u>Cain</u>." <u>British Writers</u>, ed. Ian Scott-Kilbert. Vol. IV. New York: Scribner's, 1981.

"Milton." <u>Encyclopedia Britannica</u>. 1988 ed.

Milton, John. <u>Paradise Lost</u>. New York: Odyssey, 1935.

Murray, E. B. <u>Anne Radcliffe</u>. New York: Twayne, 1972.

Natoli, Joseph. "William Blake." <u>Critical Survey of Poetry</u>. Vol. 1. Englewood Cliffs, NJ: Salem P, 1982.

Steadman, John M. <u>Milton and the Paradoxes of Renaissance Heroism</u>. Baton Rouge, LA: L.S.U.P., 1987.

Thorslev, Peter J., Jr. <u>The Byronic Hero</u>. U.S.A.: Lund, 1962.

INDEX